THE ENGLISH YEAR

THE
ENGLISH YEAR

FROM DIARIES AND
LETTERS

COMPILED BY

GEOFFREY GRIGSON

Oxford   New York

OXFORD UNIVERSITY PRESS

1984

Oxford University Press, Walton Street, Oxford OX2 6DP

London New York Toronto
Delhi Bombay Calcutta Madras Karachi
Kuala Lumpur Singapore Hong Kong Tokyo
Nairobi Dar es Salaam Cape Town
Melbourne Auckland

and associated companies in
Beirut Berlin Ibadan Mexico City Nicosia

Oxford is a trade mark of Oxford University Press

First published 1967 by Oxford University Press
First issued as an Oxford University Press paperback 1984

British Library Cataloguing in Publication Data

The English year.
1. England — Social life and customs
I. Grigson, Geoffrey
942   DA110
ISBN 0-19-281415-X

Printed in Great Britain by
The Thetford Press Ltd.
Thetford, Norfolk

I have often thought of writing a set of play-bills for the Vale of Keswick—for every day in the year—announcing each, day the performance, by his supreme Majesty's Servants, Clouds, Waters, Sun, Moon, Stars, etc.

S. T. Coleridge, 27 July 1802

Then I came back to the cottage with my throat dry thinking in what a little while I would be in my grave with the whole world lost to me.

J. M. Synge

CONTENTS

✻

ILLUSTRATIONS

*From the collection of drawings and sketches by
John Constable, in the Victoria and Albert Museum*

⇾≫ ❁ ≪↢

ACKNOWLEDGEMENTS

For permission to include various extracts thanks are due to Ralph Arnold, Esq. (diary of Richard Hayes, in *A Yeoman of Kent*); Jonathan Cape Ltd. and William Plomer, Esq. (*Kilvert's Journal*); the Oxford University Press (Jane Austen's *Letters*; *Correspondence of Thomas Gray*; Gerard Manley Hopkins's *Journal and Papers* and *Further Letters*; Ruskin's *Diaries*; Horace Walpole's *Correspondence*; *Early Letters of William and Dorothy Wordsworth*; James Woodforde's *Diary of a Country Parson*); Laurence Pollinger Ltd. and the estate of the late Frieda Lawrence (*Letters of D. H. Lawrence*); Society of Authors as the literary representative of the late Katherine Mansfield (*Letters* and *Journal* of Katherine Mansfield); Trustees of the Hardy Estate and Messrs. Macmillan (*The Life of Thomas Hardy 1840–1928*); Trustees of the Hardy Estate and the Hogarth Press (*The Notebooks of Thomas Hardy*); Routledge & Kegan Paul (*The Prose of John Clare*; *The Notebooks of Samuel Taylor Coleridge*; *Journal of Gilbert White*).

INTRODUCTION

⊷≫ ✵ ≪⊶

ENGLISH writers during the last two centuries have often
left a record in journals and in letters—an immediate
record—of observations, of something seen, something
sensed, something or other felt and enjoyed, in the
country around them, day after day, month after month,
through the year. Here then is a composite journal of the
English year chosen from such records, by poets, including
Gray and Cowper, Coleridge and Clare, Hopkins and D. H.
Lawrence; by one or two painters; and by other writers,
above all Gilbert White, watching the years, the seasons,
pass by in his Hampshire village of Selborne, Dorothy
Wordsworth, the plain gipsy-like girl watching the lakes,
fells, foxgloves, snows, stars, and reflections, and Francis
Kilvert the young clergyman who enjoyed the circumstances of Wiltshire, his native county, and Radnorshire,
the blue border of Wales, in the eighteen-seventies, with
repeated ecstasy and surprise.

I made the first selection for my own purposes, without
the idea of a book or publication, and it taught me much—
for instance, that it is not as easy as it looks to record such
notes of immediacy. It depends on exceptional power to
feel, to respond; on concentration and exclusion, on leaving out everything except the basic details which are
received into oneself most strongly and purely. And when
the annotator, or the denotator, is in form, and is not too
adjectival (which is Kilvert's amateur fault), it does seem
that he has compressed the whole natural circumstances
of life into a very few words.

The master is Dorothy Wordsworth, transmitting to us in that sense a curve of snow, a rustle of dry leaves, or the breaking of the surface of a lake between sun and mist. Her attitude always seems (though attitudes in writing of this kind are better implicit as a rule than explicit) to be one of benediction and thankfulness in a spontaneity strengthened by the added fact that she read well and by the companionship of those two poets, Coleridge and her brother, each simultaneously inhabiting thought and environment.

Such records were best before 'nature writing' became an exclusive pursuit, hardening—or softening—eventually into a mode. Here the exception comes near the beginning. Gilbert White is in a curt way the backbone of this book, of this composite year. I do not find him so different a creature from Dorothy Wordsworth, once two different concepts of nature are accounted for, nature ordered, calm, and sensible, and nature as an Earthly Paradise. 'Larches turn yellow; ash leaves fall; the hanger gets thin.' So much for autumn. 'Green wood-pecker laughs at all the world. Storm-cock sings.' So much for the third week in April. 'Swifts squeak much.' 'The water shines in the fallows.' 'Ice in the roads bears horse and man.' Gilbert White has only to be put in the right company for it to be seen that *prose* is no word for this master of the short sentence, this English miniaturist of the Floating World, regarding his Hampshire through a cool crystal eye, and writing with the fewest adjectives, and without a thought for final causes. The extracts, the sudden moments of being, chosen for the book also go back beyond the two centuries to Pepys, but like Gilbert White (or White's less known contemporary Richard Hayes), Pepys as well is far from 'prosy', so long as one thinks of poetry or perception—as one should— widely in an 'unpoetic' way. I was going to add that the reader will find an admixture of records which really are of a plainer kind, keeping the seasons of the year in motion, from New Year's Day to New Year's Eve: it was mainly that Norfolk rector James Woodforde I was thinking of, so much given to noting meals he immensely consumed, so encased in a non-conducting hide that he only noticed the day or the night, as a rule, when extremest conditions interfered with the larder or his comfort. Yet there is to be found even in Woodforde, in spite of himself, a little of the peculiar melodies of existence.

So much for one way of reading this book, for gladness or for its union with sadness (read the young Coleridge recording the same evening how—on 25 July—he and the Wordsworths had drunk tea on the island in Grasmere and then danced by the light of their bonfire of fir-cones, read elderly Cowper watching the yellow leaves falling everywhere— 26 October—and wishing, after all, in spite of his old Evangelical conviction that a short life is better in this world of wickedness, to 'live and live always').

There is another way of reading this *English Year*, and one which will give additional pleasure—making it a weather book, a day book, reading it by the calendar, discovering from it repeatedly what to-day was like *then*— comparing to-days; discovering past time (and past response) crystallized in language. So after each item of this composite year I have given the actual year of the record, and the county or district where it was made. I have still called the book *The English Year*, though the eye falls often enough outside the strict boundaries of England. But then it was usually an English eye; and the words its images evoked are English.

As for illustrations, it struck me that the best way of illustrating an English year was through one man rather than many—through the one major artist of the English school who has left enough drawings and sketches directly responding to the seasons (and one who contributes also in words). Constable dated most of his drawings, obligingly; or perhaps, when it comes to selecting one drawing or sketch for each of the twelve months, a little disobligingly.

He was not one to be about very often, or at least to be out and drawing, in the wintrier months, when there were pictures to be composed for the year's exhibition. He was not a painter for snow or stars or crescent moons. And he admired Gilbert White—though he was also moved by torn black skies and storms. But if the drawings do not all hit the month exactly, they come near to it, they hit the season.

The first drawing, *Fir Trees at Hampstead Heath*, serves here for the New Year, at any rate for the evergreen in winter, though Constable made the drawing in October, on the fourth anniversary of his wedding day. In a curious way it illustrates the meeting of those poles of fact and vision which are the substance of this book—of intensified fact and Earthly Paradise. I have always supposed it to be this drawing which excited praise from William Blake, according to the anecdote in Leslie's *Life of Constable*: 'The aimiable but eccentric Blake, looking through one of Constable's sketchbooks, said of a beautiful drawing of an avenue of fir trees on Hampstead Heath, "Why, this is not drawing, but *inspiration*"; and he replied—sensible if cutting admirer of the calm sunshine of the heart—"I never knew it before; I meant it for drawing."'

The pines grew, I think, on one of the knolls across from the Bull and Bush; and it was perhaps at Collin's Farm—the modern Wildes—behind the Bull and Bush, that Blake and Constable met, and Blake looked through the sketchbook.

Geoffrey Grigson

JANUARY

⇝❋⇜

JANUARY 1

Lay long, being a bitter, cold, frosty day, the frost being now grown old, & the Thames covered with ice.
Samuel Pepys, 1667 (London)

It freezes under people's beds.
Gilbert White, 1768 (Hampshire)

Oak leaves a sober silver grey on their backs.
S. T. Coleridge, 1804 (Westmorland)

The country was wrapped in one vast winding sheet of snow, the roads were dumb . . . no sound but the swift sharp rustle of the driving snow in the hedges and hollies.
Francis Kilvert, 1875 (Wiltshire)

JANUARY 2

Cold weather brings out upon the faces of people the written marks of their habits, vices, passions, and memories, as warmth brings out on paper a writing in sympathetic ink.
Thomas Hardy, 1886 (Dorset)

JANUARY 3

Remember to describe water . . pulsating, really gliding down under ice, water—black under ice, silver.
S. T. Coleridge, 1804 (Westmorland)

After a very bright day, the air rinsed quite clear, there was a slash of glowing, yolk-coloured sunset.

Gerard Manley Hopkins, 1869 (Surrey)

JANUARY 4

Our roads are very full of water, I never saw the London turnpike so much cut with the carriages, by having almost continuous rains, little or much.

Richard Hayes, 1764 (Kent)

Rain, rain. Gleams. Venus is very resplendent.

Gilbert White, 1793 (Hampshire)

Horsedung echoing to the merry (Foot-) traveller on a frosty morning.   *S. T. Coleridge, 1804 (Westmorland)*

Woke early and saw a snowy branch across the window. It is cold, snow has fallen, and now it is thawing. . . . Very dark, too, with a wind somewhere.

Katherine Mansfield, 1915 (Buckinghamshire)

JANUARY 5

Snow on the ground—snatched up by the wind that full of frosty particles seemed to rush from the valley up the mountain, it galloped transversely from the middlemost of the mountains to their very top, and along their summits, like a vast ghost cavalry scouring a country. Item, I distinctly and repeatedly saw the wind raise up from the mountain a true genuine cloud of snow, that rose high . . . sailed along, a true genuine large white cloud with all the form and varied outline of a cloud—and this in several instances dropped again, snow at second hand, and often in the sun resembled a shower of diamond spearlets.

S. T. Coleridge, 1804 (Westmorland)

There have been great winds, and the sea has been smoking white above the cliff—such a wind that it made one laugh with astonishment. Now it is still again, and the evening is very yellow. *D. H. Lawrence, 1916 (Cornwall)*

Saw the sun rise. A lovely apricot sky with flames in it and then a solemn pink. Heavens, how beautiful! I heard a knocking, and went downstairs. It was Benny cutting away the ivy. Over the path lay the fallen nests—wisps of hay and feathers. He looked like an ivy bush himself. I made early tea and carried it up to J., who lay half awake with crinkled eyes. I feel so full of love to-day after having seen the sun rise.

Katherine Mansfield, 1915 (Buckinghamshire)

JANUARY 6

Old Christmas Day. Last night the slip of the Holy Thorn ... grafted for me last spring in the Vicarage lower garden blossomed in an intense frost.

Frances Kilvert, 1879 (Herefordshire)

JANUARY 7

Shook the snow from the ever-greens, and shovelled the walks. *Gilbert White, 1785 (Hampshire)*

5.40 p.m. . . . A sublime sort of evening—windy, vast, with wild clouds and great spreads of mournful light where the sun had been, clearing away for a while into a starry purple dome, with the Pleiades and Orion and the Great Bear and the Galaxy, a sight that makes man feel his immortality

and his littleness more than perhaps any other . . . Across
the pale amber two or three dark, almost black, little
clouds drove slanting like collapsing balloons. Against this
western screen the trees showed their leafless fringes, and a
bend of the New River lay gloomy and blue beneath them.

James Smetham, 1861 (Middlesex)

JANUARY 8

Bushes and short trees blown like the flame of a candle.
Long-tailed tits on dead stems of willow herb 4 ft. high.
Rushes, half dead, half green.

Never go for a walk in the fields without seeing one thing
at least however small to give me hope, the frond of a
fern among dead leaves.   *Richard Jefferies, 1884 (Sussex)*

JANUARY 9

Rooks resort to their nest-trees. Hepaticas, winter-aconite,
wall-flowers, daiseys, polyanths, black hellebores blow.
Wheat looks well on the downs.

Gilbert White, 1769 (Hampshire)

JANUARY 10

The arum just appearing under the hedges as in April; and
the Avens . . . has never lost its leaves but appears as green
as at Spring.   *John Clare, 1825 (Northants)*

JANUARY 11

Brisk wind but quite warm. Song thrush pipes away as
though an April morn.   *Richard Hayes, 1765 (Kent)*

The air early this morning was as warm as the air of a hot-house and the thrushes singing like mad thinking that spring had come. *Francis Kilvert, 1872 (Wiltshire)*

JANUARY 12

When I came out the night was superb. The sky was cloudless, the moon rode high and full in the deep blue vault and the evening star blazed in the west. The air was filled with the tolling and chiming of bells from St Paul's and Chippenham old Church. . . . I walked up and down the drive several times before I could make up my mind to leave the wonderful beauty of the night and go indoors.

Francis Kilvert, 1873 (Wiltshire)

JANUARY 13

The earth is glutted with water: rills break out at the foot of every little hill: my well is nearly half full. The wind in the night blew down the rain-measurer.

Gilbert White, 1791 (Hampshire)

JANUARY 14

Rugged, Siberian weather. The narrow lanes are full of snow in some places. . . . The road-waggons are obliged to stop, and the stage-coaches are much embarassed. I was obliged to be much abroad on this day, and scarce ever saw its fellow. *Gilbert White, 1776 (Hampshire)*

The season so remarkably mild and warm that my brother gathered this morning in my garden some full blown primroses. *James Woodforde, 1790 (Norfolk)*

7

JANUARY 15

This evening there was the most perfect and the brightest halo circling the roundest and brightest moon I have ever beheld. So bright was the halo, so compact, so entire a circle, that it gave the whole of its area, the moon itself included, the appearance of a solid opaque body, an enormous planet.　　　*S. T. Coleridge, 1805 (Westmorland)*

JANUARY 16

I stayed up till the bell-man came by with his bell just under my window as I was writing of this very line, and cried, 'Past one of the clock, and a cold, frosty, windy morning.'
Samuel Pepys, 1660 (Westminster)

Severe air. Icicles. Cutting wind and frost.
Gilbert White, 1772 (Hampshire)

JANUARY 17

To-day dark, and railroad whistles shrill.
John Ruskin, 1872 (Denmark Hill, Surrey)

JANUARY 18

I took a walk to Kentish-Town, wind N.W., bright and frosty. Thermometer at Noon was at 42. The grass remarkably green and flourishing. I observed, on dry banks facing the south that Chickweed, Dandelion, Groundsel, Red Archangel, and Shepherd's Purse were beginning to flower. This is all I know of the Country.
Thomas Grey, 1761 (Middlesex)

The elms are hung and beaded with round buds and many
trees have the Spring smoky claret colour.
>   *Gerard Manley Hopkins, 1873 (Hampstead)*

JANUARY 19

Down early. The twilight is bright now at seven and was
clear, last evening, through the cedar at five.
>   *John Ruskin, 1872 (Denmark Hill, Surrey)*

Coming back from Talbothays by West Stafford Cross I saw
Orion upside-down in a pool of water under an oak.
>   *Thomas Hardy, 1920 (Dorset)*

JANUARY 20

Lambs fall,[1] and are frozen to the ground.
>   *Gilbert White, 1775 (Hampshire)*

The trees and the clouds seem to ask me to try and do
something like them.   *John Constable, 1834 (Hampstead)*

A man outside is breaking stones. The day is utterly quiet.
Sometimes a leaf rustles and a strange puff of wind passes
the window. The old man chops, chops, as though it were a
heart beating out there.
>   *Katherine Mansfield, 1915 (Buckinghamshire)*

JANUARY 21

As mild a day as though May. N.B. I saw a spotted butterfly—brown colour.   *Richard Hayes, 1762 (Kent)*

---

[1] i.e. are born.

Sunday. A cold raw frost fog, dark and dreary . . . the Chapel bell tolled out sharp and sudden through the white mist to give notice of the service a quarter of an hour beforehand. The hedges were hoary with rime and frost and the trees were hailing large pieces of ice down into the road.

Few people in Chapel. . . . I thought the markers in the Bible and Prayers had suddenly become very short, and after service Wilding the Clerk told me the church mice had eaten them off.   *Francis Kilvert, 1872 (Radnorshire)*

JANUARY 22

Ice in the roads bears horse and man. Vast halo round the moon.   *Gilbert White, 1769 (Hampshire)*

Brother dined with us. Neck of pork roasted. He put the blind down a little while. Sun began to weaken the fire.
    Richard Hayes, 1778 (Kent)

JANUARY 23

It rained all the way home. We struggled with the wind, and often rested as we went along. A hail shower met us before we reached the Tarn, and the way often was difficult over the snow; but at the Tarn the view closed in. We saw nothing but mists and snow: and at first the ice on the Tarn below us cracked and split, yet without water, a dull grey white. . . . There was no footmark upon the snow either of man or beast. We saw 4 sheep before we had left the snow region.   *Dorothy Wordsworth, 1802 (Westmorland)*

JANUARY 24

Sky strangely streaked with blue and red. Wind and rain in the night. Larks rise and essay to sing. Daws begin to come to churches.   *Gilbert White, 1771 (Hampshire)*

The sky spread over with one continuous cloud, whitened by the light of the moon, which, though her dim shape was seen, did not throw forth so strong a light as to chequer the earth with shadows. At once the clouds seemed to cleave asunder, and left her in the centre of a black-blue vault. She sailed along, followed by multitudes of stars, small, and bright, and sharp. Their brightness seemed concentrated (half-moon).   *Dorothy Wordsworth, 1798 (Somerset)*

How do you like this cold weather? I hope you have all been earnestly praying for it as a salutary relief from the dreadfully mild and unhealthy season preceding it, fancying yourself half putrified from the want of it, and that you now all draw into the fire, complain that you never felt such bitterness of cold before, that you are half starved, quite frozen, and wish the mild weather back again with all your hearts.   *Jane Austen, 1801 (Hampshire)*

A fine day. The bees were busily flying as if seeking flowers, the sky was hung with light flying clouds and the season appeared as if the beginning of April.
          John Clare, 1825 (Northants)

A beautiful gleam of sunshine lit the rainy mountains into tender showery lights of blue and green.
          Francis Kilvert, 1872 (Radnorshire)

JANUARY 26

Walked upon the hill-tops; followed the sheep tracks till we overlooked the larger coombe. Sat in the sunshine. The distant sheep-bells, the sound of the stream; the woodman winding along the half-marked road with his laden pony; locks of wool still spangled with the dew-drops; the blue-grey sea, shaded with immense masses of cloud, not streaked; the sheep glittering in the sunshine.

Dorothy Wordsworth, 1798 (Somerset)

JANUARY 27

A beautiful mild morning; the sun shone; the lake was still, and all the shores reflected in it. . . . The bees were humming about the hive. William raked a few stones off the garden, his first garden labour this year. I cut the shrubs.   *Dorothy Wordsworth, 1802 (Westmorland)*

JANUARY 28

On the Downs. . . . I opened my eyes again, and saw it was daytime. And I saw the sea lifted up and shining like a blade with the sun on it. And high up, on the icy wind, an aeroplane flew towards us from the land—and the men ploughing and the boys in the fields on the table-lands, and the shepherds, stood back from their work and lifted their faces. And the aeroplane was small and high, in the thin, ice-cold wind. And the birds became silent and dashed to cover, afraid of the noise. And the aeroplane floated high out of sight. And below, on the level earth away down—were floods and stretches of snow, and I knew I was awake.

D. H. Lawrence, 1915 (Sussex)

JANUARY 29

To Southwark, and so over the fields to Lambeth, and there drank, it being a most glorious and warm day, even to amazement, for this time of the year.

Samuel Pepys, 1661 (Surrey)

It was a mild afternoon. There was an unusual softness in the prospects as we went, a rich yellow upon the fields, and a soft grave purple on the waters. When we returned many stars were out, the clouds were moveless, in the sky soft purple, the lake of Rydale calm, Jupiter behind. Jupiter at least *we* call him, but William says we always call the largest star Jupiter.

Dorothy Wordsworth, 1802 (Westmorland)

JANUARY 30

My lot is cast in a country where we have neither woods nor commons, nor pleasant prospects; all flat and insipid; in the summer adorned only with blue willows, and in the winter covered with a flood. Such it is at present: our bridges shaken almost in pieces; our poor willows torn away by the roots, and our haycocks almost afloat. Yet even here we are happy.

William Cowper, 1767 (Huntingdonshire)

JANUARY 31

So thick a fog, could not see my Obelisk.

Richard Hayes, 1771 (Kent)

A yellow crocus and a bunch of single snowdrops in full flower—the mavis thrush has been singing all day long. Spring seems begun. The woodbines all over the wood are in full leaf.

John Clare, 1825 (Northants)

The first day, this year, begun without candles. Birds singing a little.

John Ruskin, 1884 (Coniston, Lancashire)

FEBRUARY

FEBRUARY 1

The wind blew so keen in our faces that we felt ourselves
inclined to seek the covert of the wood. There we had a
warm shelter, gathered a burthen of rotten boughs blown
down by the wind of the preceding night. The sun shone
clear, but all at once a heavy blackness hung over the sea.
The trees almost *roared*, and the ground seemed in motion
with the multitudes of dancing leaves, which made a
rustling sound, distinct from that of the trees. Still the asses
pastured in quietness under the hollies. . . . The wind beat
furiously against us as we returned. Full moon. She rose in
uncommon majesty over the sea, slowly ascending through
the clouds. Sat with the window open an hour in the
moonlight.   *Dorothy Wordsworth, 1798 (Somerset)*

Very hard frost with much snow and very rough easterly
wind. . . . I don't know that I ever felt a more severe day.
The turnips all froze to blocks, obliged to split them with
beetle and wedges, and some difficulty to get at them on
account of the snow—their tops entirely gone and they lay
as apples on the ground.
          James Woodforde, 1799 (Norfolk)

There is a glimpse of sun. The trees look as though they
were hanging out to dry.
          Katherine Mansfield, 1915 (Buckinghamshire)

The morning was superb, warm, and brilliant, like a May morning, and the hundreds of yellow stars of the Cape jessamine between the drawing room and dining room windows were full of bees.

Francis Kilvert, 1872 (Radnorshire)

Gathered sticks in the wood; a perfect stillness. The redbreasts sang upon the leafless boughs. Of a great number of sheep in the field, only one standing. Returned to dinner at five o'clock. The moonlight still and warm as a summer's night at nine o'clock.

Dorothy Wordsworth, 1798 (Somerset)

The first winter's day. A sharp frost and a night fall of snow drifted in heaps by a keen wind. There has been a deal of talk about the forwardness of this season.

John Clare, 1825 (Northants)

As cold a night last night almost as we have had yet, it froze very sharp within doors, all the milk and cream froze. Extreme cold this morning with cutting wind, and much snow besides . . . the rooks and crows so tame that they come up to the kitchen door where I feed my poultry. Dinner to day, boiled veal and pork, etc.

James Woodforde, 1795 (Norfolk)

The coloured primroses were in full bloom in the little round garden plots under the windows. As I came down the hill the air was cold, it had turned cold suddenly, and I noticed that the sky was wild and stormy, bright and tumbled. *Francis Kilvert, 1872 (Radnorshire)*

FEBRUARY 5

Frost, sun, yellow evening.
Gilbert White, 1774 (Hampshire)

Out after dinner—bright stars—half-moon—frost in the morning. Aconite in flower, hazels hung with green catkins.
William Allingham, 1887 (Surrey)

FEBRUARY 6

Frost, sun, fog, rain, snow.
Gilbert White, 1771 (Hampshire)

Foxes begin now to be very rank, and to smell so high, that as one rides along of a morning it is easy to distinguish where they have been the night before. At this season the intercourse between the sexes commences.
Gilbert White, 1778 (Hampshire)

Another fairy frost. The rime froze on the trees during the night and this morning every bough was bearded with the delicate frost work. *Francis Kilvert, 1874 (Wiltshire)*

FEBRUARY 7

By the Chaffinches beginning to chaunt, their notes put me in mind of birdsnesting as I rode to Dartford.
Richard Hayes, 1778 (Kent)

A fine clear frosty morning. The eaves drop with the heat of the sun all day long. The ground thinly covered with snow. The road black, rocks bluish. Before night the island [on Grasmere] was quite green. The sun had melted all the snow upon it.

Dorothy Wordsworth, 1802 (Westmorland)

It was a beautiful day here to-day, with bright, new, wide-opened sunshine, and lovely new scents in the fresh air, as if new blood were rising. And the sea came in great long waves thundering splendidly from the unknown. It is perfect, with a strong, pure wind blowing. What does it matter about that seething scrimmage of mankind in Europe? If that were indeed the only truth, one might indeed despair.

D. H. Lawrence, 1916 (Cornwall)

FEBRUARY 8

Venus *shadows* very strongly, showing the bars of the windows on the floors and walls.

Gilbert White, 1782 (Hampshire)

FEBRUARY 9

It is marvellous weather—brilliant sunshine on the snow, clear as summer, slightly golden sun, distance lit up. But it is immensely cold—everything frozen solid—milk, mustard, everything. Yesterday I went out for a real walk—I've had a cold and been in bed. I climbed with my niece to the bare top of the hills. Wonderful it is to see the foot-marks on the snow—beautiful ropes of rabbit prints, trailing away over the brows; heavy hare marks; a fox so sharp and dainty, going over the wall: birds with two feet that hop; very splendid straight advance of a pheasant; wood-pigeons that are clumsy and move in flocks; splendid little leaping marks of weasels coming along like a necklace chain of berries; odd little filagree of the field-mice; the trail of a mole—it is astonishing what a world of wild creatures one feels about one, on the hills in snow.

D. H. Lawrence, 1919 (Derbyshire)

FEBRUARY 10

In spite of myself I cannot help noticing countenances and tempers in objects of scenery, e.g. trees, hills, houses.

Thomas Hardy, 1897 (Dorset)

FEBRUARY 11

Coltsfoot in flower, embankment. Goldfinch brilliant wings seen from above, perched stalk of wild carrot. Larks on ground, song in short bursts, like springs of water in meadow.

Richard Jefferies, 1883 (Sussex)

FEBRUARY 12

Daffodils have been in bloom for some days. A weeping-willow here is all green. The elms have long been in red bloom, and yesterday I saw small leaves on the brushwood at their roots. Some primroses out.

Gerard Manley Hopkins, 1869 (Surrey)

The slate slabs of the urinals even are frosted in graceful sprays.

Gerard Manley Hopkins, 1870 (Surrey)

FEBRUARY 13

The baby was baptized in ice which was broken and swimming about in the font.

Francis Kilvert, 1879 (Radnorshire)

FEBRUARY 14

Gathered sticks with William in the wood, he being unwell and not able to go further. The young birch trees of a bright red, through which gleams a shade of purple. Sat down in a thick part of the wood. The near trees still, even to their topmost boughs, but a perpetual motion in those that skirt the wood. The breeze rose gently; its path distinctly marked, till it came to the very spot where we were. *Dorothy Wordsworth, 1798 (Somerset)*

FEBRUARY 15

Snow deep and drifted thro' the hedges in curious, and romantic shapes. *Gilbert White, 1784 (Hampshire)*

Here the winds are so black and terrible. They rush with such force that the house shudders, though the old walls are very solid and thick. Only occasionally the gulls rise very slowly into the air. And all the while the wind rushes and thuds and booms, and all the while the sea is hoarse and heavy. It is strange, one forgets the rest of life. It shuts one in within its massive violent world. Sometimes a wave bursts with a great explosion against one of the outlying rocks, and there is a tremendous ghost standing high on the sea, a great tall whiteness. *D. H. Lawrence, 1916 (Cornwall)*

FEBRUARY 16

A perfect, quiet, intensely bright sky with silver, silent clouds all day. *John Ruskin, 1868 (Denmark Hill, Surrey)*

FEBRUARY 17

A deep snow upon the ground. . . . We walked through the wood into the Coombe to fetch some eggs. The sun shone bright and clear. A deep stillness in the thickest part of the wood, undisturbed except by the occasional dropping of the snow from the holly boughs; no other sound but that of the water, and the slender notes of a redbreast, which sang at intervals on the outskirts of the southern side of the wood. There the bright green moss was bare at the roots of the trees, and the little birds were upon it . . . each tree taken singly was beautiful. The branches of the hollies pendent with their white burden, but still showing their bright red berries, and their glossy green leaves. The bare branches of the oaks thickened by the snow.

Dorothy Wordsworth, 1798 (Somerset)

FEBRUARY 18

Pleasant season: paths dry. Men plough and sow. Large titmouse sings his three notes.

Gilbert White, 1786 (Hampshire)

Very hard frost with strong easterly winds, a black frost. . . . Had a fire again in my bedchamber to-night.

James Woodforde, 1795 (Norfolk)

FEBRUARY 19

The moon and Venus in the S.W. and Jupiter and Mars in the E. make nightly a charming appearance.

Gilbert White, 1790 (Hampshire)

FEBRUARY 20

Truffles continue to be found in my brother Henry's grove of beeches: tho' the season is near at an end. It is supposed that seven or eight pounds are taken annually at that little spot. My brother and the truffle-hunter divide them equally between them.   *Gilbert White, 1773 (Hampshire)*

The Sky Lark now begins to usher in the spring, by piping
his melodious note aloft in the sky.

Richard Hayes, 1774 (Kent)

FEBRUARY 21

A very wet morning. . . . Snowdrops quite out, but cold and
winterly; yet, for all this, a thrush that lives in our orchard
has shouted and sung its merriest all day long.

Dorothy Wordsworth, 1802 (Cumberland)

What a lovely thing a bit of fine, sharp, crystallised broken
snow is, held up against the blue sky catching the sun—
talk of diamonds!

John Ruskin, 1843 (Denmark Hill, Surrey)

FEBRUARY 22

After luncheon went for a walk . . . to the top of Drum du.
When we got to the cairn Plynlimmon was quite visible,
but only the ghost of Cader Idris to be seen. We went away
disappointed but had not gone far before the clouds suddenly lifted and a sun burst lit up grandly the great snow-
slopes of round-backed Plynlimmon and the vast snowy
precipices of the giant Cader Idris near 50 miles away.

Francis Kilvert, 1870 (Radnorshire)

FEBRUARY 23

I observe now Spring begins by my Crocusses and Crown
Pearls under hall window, with yellow rose budding for
leaf.   *Richard Hayes, 1773 (Kent)*

A lunar halo: I looked at it from the upstairs library
window. It was a grave grained sky. . . . The halo was not

quite round, for in the first place it was a little pulled and drawn below, by the refraction of the lower air perhaps, but what is more it fell in on the nether left hand side, which was not quite at full. I could not but strongly feel in my fancy the odd instress of this, the moon leaning on her side, as if fallen back, in the cheerful light floor within the ring, after with magical rightness and success tracing round her the ring, the steady copy of her own outline. But this sober grey darkness and pale light was happily broken through by the orange of the pealing of Mitton bells.

Gerard Manley Hopkins, 1872 (Lancashire)

FEBRUARY 24

. . . The sea, like a basin full to the margin; the dark fresh-ploughed fields; the turnips of a lively rough green.

Dorothy Wordsworth, 1798 (Somerset)

The Black Mountain lighted up grandly, all the furrows and watercourses clear and brilliant. People coming home from market, birds singing, buds bursting, and the spring air full of beauty, life and hope.

Francis Kilvert, 1870 (Radnorshire)

Just at present it is very cold. It has been blowing here also, and a bit of snow. Till now the weather has been so mild. Primroses and violets are out, and the gorse is lovely. At Zennor one sees infinite Atlantic, all peacock-mingled colours, and the gorse is sunshine itself, already. But this cold wind is deadly.   *D. H. Lawrence, 1916 (Cornwall)*

FEBRUARY 25

Gnats fly, and large flies. Mezereon flowers.

Thomas Gray, 1763 (Cambridge)

Rowed to Fir Island, the beauty of it and intense quiet making me feel as if in a feverish dream. A robin met and waited by me, at each of the two places where I landed, and flitted from stone to stone at the water's edge.

John Ruskin, 1873 (Coniston Lake, Lancashire)

FEBRUARY 26

A winter prospect shows every cottage, every farm, and the forms of distant trees, such as in summer have no distinguishing mark.

Dorothy Wordsworth, 1798 (Somerset)

FEBRUARY 27

The sea big and white, swelled to the very shores, but round and high in the middle. Coleridge returned with me, as far as the wood. A very bright moonlight night. Venus almost like another moon. Lost to us at Alfoxden long before she goes down (into) the large white sea.

Dorothy Wordsworth, 1798 (Somerset)

How misty is England! I have spent four years in a gray gloom. And yet it suits me pretty well.

Nathaniel Hawthorne, 1857 (Lancashire)

FEBRUARY 28

What an interval! Heard the singing birds this morning in our garden for the first time this year, though it rained and blew fiercely; but the long frost has broken up, and the wind, though fierce, was warm and westerly.

S. T. Coleridge, 1827 (Highgate)

FEBRUARY 29

I saw some blessed purple walls against sunshine among the farms, and seemed to find my life again on the green banks.

John Ruskin, 1876 (Oxfordshire)

MARCH

✦

MARCH 1

The shapes of the mist, slowly moving along, exquisitely beautiful; passing over the sheep they almost seemed to have more of life than those quiet creatures. The unseen birds singing in the mist.

Dorothy Wordsworth, 1798 (Somerset)

Wild wind and rain and hail.

Francis Kilvert, 1876 (Wiltshire)

MARCH 2

Dull and damp. At night sky swept with mare's-tail clouds in bold strange comet shapes, stars scattered, Venus—now very bright—with a watery nimbus and like a lamp, moon with a milky-blue iris.

Gerard Manley Hopkins, 1868 (Warwickshire)

The birds are singing, and the garden is full of clumps of snowdrops. I meant to enclose some but I find they look wretched against white paper.

Gerard Manley Hopkins, 1871 (Lancashire)

The sun a vast bulb of crimson pulp.

Thomas Hardy, 1879 (Dorset)

MARCH 3

Dull. A green daylight in the hedges. Lilac trees have big green buds.

Gerard Manley Hopkins, 1868 (Warwickshire)

MARCH 4

Sunday. I went for a walk this morning, and discovered that spring had come.

Not at first. Grey drifts of cloud overhead; and a biting east wind. . . . Somewhere in Sandy Lane I saw the snow-white glossy tips of palm-buds. A little further on, the lush green of a young arum leaf. It is strange how these leaves appear suddenly, you don't know how or when.

Expecting to see celandine in some sheltered corner, I walked on but a few yards; then pulled up before a mole working.   *George Sturt, 1900 (Surrey)*

MARCH 5

Vast icicles on eaves.   *Gilbert White, 1786 (Hampshire)*

The moon hung over the northern side of the highest point of Silver How, like a gold ring snapped in two, and shaven off at the ends, it was so narrow. Within this ring lay the circle of the Round Moon, as *distinctly* to be seen as ever the enlightened moon is.

Dorothy Wordsworth, 1802 (Westmorland)

MARCH 6

A sudden and blessed change in the weather, a S.W. wind, bearing warm rain, and the birds in the garden and orchard singing like mad creatures.

Francis Kilvert, 1875 (Wiltshire)

MARCH 7

Snow drifted over hedges and gates. . . . Blackbirds and thrushes die. . . . As Mr Ventris came from Faringdon, the drifted snow, being hard-frozen, bore his weight up to the tops of the stiles. The net hung over the cherry trees is curiously coated over with ice.

Gilbert White, 1786 (Hampshire)

Now there is no bird sings so persistently in every copse and indeed every garden as that which cries Teejum-Teejum every day. View of the Tomtit who reminds us of the tidum tijum of life till we dislike him.

Richard Jefferies, 1885 (Kent)

MARCH 8

The crocuses make a gaudy appearance, and bees gather on them. The air is soft. Violets blow. Snow lies under hedges. Men plow.   *Gilbert White, 1783 (Hampshire)*

It is still cold. Snow falls sometimes, then vanishes at once. When the sun shines, some gorse bushes smell hot and sweet.   *D. H. Lawrence, 1916 (Cornwall)*

MARCH 9

Very pleasant sunny warm day. My rooks for the week past have been very busy a building. And the butterflies have turned out. Crocuses and spring flowers appear. I now look upon this to be the pleasantest time of the year.

Richard Hayes, 1766 (Kent)

This morning, the world was white with snow. This evening the sunset is yellow, the birds are whistling, the gorse bushes are bristling with little winged suns. . . . The new incoming days seem most wonderful, uncreated.

D. H. Lawrence, 1916 (Cornwall)

MARCH 10

In the lane below Pen y fforest a storm cock sat singing in the top of a tree, a song that sounded as if a man were playing upon a flageolet, and the bird was not wrong in his presage, for before I gained the Cwm a black snow cloud drove suddenly up from the North West and over-spread the pale clear blue sky, and the whirling driving snowstorm swept down the dingle and hid the tops of the hills. *Francis Kilvert, 1873 (Radnorshire)*

MARCH 11

The frogs have begun to croak and spawn in the ponds and dykes. *John Clare, 1825 (Northants)*

MARCH 12

The sun shone while it rained, and the stones of the walls and the pebbles on the road glittered like silver.
Dorothy Wordsworth, 1802 (Westmorland)

MARCH 13

After dinner we walked to Rydale for letters—it was terribly cold—we had 2 or 3 brisk hail showers—the hail stones looked clean and pretty upon the dry clean road. Little Peggy Simpson was standing at the door catching the hail stones in her hand.
Dorothy Wordsworth, 1802 (Westmorland)

MARCH 14

Papilio rhamni, the brimstone butterfly, appears in the Holt. Trouts rise, and catch at insects. A dob-chick comes down the Wey in sight of the windows, some times diving, and some times running on the banks. Timothy the tortoise comes forth, and weighs 6 lbs. $5\frac{1}{2}$ oz.

Gilbert White, 1793 (Hampshire)

My double scarlet anemonie in full flower—A sharp frosty morning. *John Clare, 1825 (Northants)*

MARCH 15

Fine and summer-like. . . . Chervil and woodsorrel out. Hawthorn sprays papered with young leaves.—Venus like an apple of light.

Gerard Manley Hopkins, 1868 (Warwickshire)

MARCH 16

As I passed Cross Fford the frogs were croaking, snoring and bubbling in the pool under the full moon.

Francis Kilvert, 1870 (Radnorshire)

MARCH 17

Nuthatch brings out and cracks her nuts, and strews the garden walks with shells. They fix them in a fork of a tree where two boughs meet—on the Orleans plum tree.

Gilbert White, 1775 (Hampshire)

Green plovers on the common. The uncrested wren, the smallest species, called in this place the *Chif-chaf*, is very loud in the Lythe. This is the earliest bird of passage, and the harbinger of spring.   *Gilbert White, 1780 (Hampshire)*

The Coleridges left us. A cold, windy morning. Walked with them half way. On our return, sheltered under the hollies, during a hail-shower. The withered leaves danced with the hailstones. *Dorothy Wordsworth, 1798 (Somerset)*

Rydale vale was full of life and motion. The wind blew briskly, and the lake was covered all over with bright silver waves, that were there each the twinkling of an eye, then others rose up and took their place as fast as they went away. The rooks glittered in the sunshine, the crows and the ravens were busy, and the thrushes and little birds sang. I went through the fields, and sat $\frac{1}{2}$ an hour afraid to pass a Cow. The Cow looked at me, and I looked at the Cow, and whenever I stirred the Cow gave over eating.

Dorothy Wordsworth, 1802 (Westmorland)

Desperately cold, with huge-flaked snow. The worst of January, November and March all in one.

John Ruskin, 1867 (Denmark Hill, Surrey)

The sun was almost overpowering. Heavy black clouds drove up and rolled round the sky without veiling the hot sunshine, black clouds with white edges they were, looking suspiciously like thunder clouds. Against these black clouds the sunshine showed the faint delicate green and pink of the trees thickening with bursting buds.

Francis Kilvert, 1871 (Radnorshire)

MARCH 20

A very cold evening, but clear. The spring seemingly very little advanced. No green trees, only the hedges are budding, and looking very lovely.

Dorothy Wordsworth, 1798 (Somerset)

MARCH 21

This day I saw a yellow butterfly. . . . My rooks, by the cold weather and snows, did not begin building till last Sunday (14th). *Richard Hayes, 1762 (Kent)*

Earthworms lie out, and copulate.

Gilbert White, 1775 (Hampshire)

We drank tea at Coleridge's. A quiet shower of snow was in the air during more than half our walk.

Dorothy Wordsworth, 1798 (Somerset)

MARCH 22

Wheat-fields look naked like fallows. The surface of the ground is all dust. *Gilbert White, 1785 (Hampshire)*

MARCH 23

Crown imperials bud for bloom, and stink much.

Gilbert White, 1792 (Hampshire)

Coleridge dined with us. He brought his ballad finished [*The Rime of the Ancyent Marinere*]. We walked with him to the Miner's house. A beautiful evening, very starry, the horned moon. *Dorothy Wordsworth, 1798 (Somerset)*

MARCH 24

A mighty cold and windy but clear day and had the pleasure of seeing the Medway running, winding up and down mightily, and a very fine country.

Samuel Pepys, 1669 (Kent)

A duller night than the last: a sort of white shade over the blue sky. The stars dim. The spring continues to advance very slowly, no green trees, the hedges leafless; nothing green but the brambles that still retain their old leaves, the evergreens, and the palms, which indeed are not absolutely green. Some brambles I observed to-day budding afresh, and those have shed their old leaves. The crooked arm of the old oak tree points upwards to the moon.

Dorothy Wordsworth, 1798 (Somerset)

A snowy Palm Sunday. Snow on the Palms. . . . I saw what I thought was a long dazzling white and golden cloud up in the sky. Suddenly I found that I had been gazing at the great snow slopes of the Black Mountain lit up by the setting sun and looking through the dark storm clouds.

Francis Kilvert, 1872 (Radnorshire)

MARCH 25

Chaffinches pull off the finest flowers of the polyanths.

Gilbert White, 1790 (Hampshire)

MARCH 26

Blade leaves of some bulbous plant, perhaps a small iris, were like delicate little saws, so hagged with frost.

Gerard Manley Hopkins, 1872 (Lancashire)

Good Friday. Rain all night. Sullen and ugly clouds on hills this morning, the black wind blowing them across from the west, though on the lake the waves move from the south. Leaves trembling, and sky one universal grey above the clouds. Robins twittering a little.

John Ruskin, 1875 (Coniston, Lancashire)

MARCH 27

A clear afternoon, with some beauty of amber light behind hills, and lovely starlight at ten, changed instantly into whistling wild wind at $\frac{1}{2}$ past 10, and this morning rain, bitter cold black wind and wild lake, all blowing from the south. I utterly languid and cold handed and hopeless.　　　*John Ruskin, 1875 (Coniston, Lancashire)*

MARCH 28

Softest quiet poised clouds, calm lake in sunshine, the sound of streams from hills, and the sense of peaceful power in all things.　　　*John Ruskin, 1886 (Coniston, Lancashire)*

MARCH 29

Deeply dark without wind. . . . Almonds all bitten to death.

John Ruskin, 1876 (Herne Hill, Surrey)

MARCH 30

Papilio rhamni [Brimstone Butterfly] sucks the bloom of the primrose. Polyanths coddled with the frost.

Gilbert White, 1770 (Hampshire)

Black weather. Cucumber fruit swells. Rooks sit. This day the dry weather has lasted a month.

Gilbert White, 1768 (Hampshire)

The face of the earth naked to a surprising degree. Wheat hardly to be seen, and no signs of any grass: turneps all gone, and sheep in a starving way. All provisions rising in price. Farmers cannot sow for want of rain.

Gilbert White, 1771 (Hampshire)

Rain at last after weeks of the driest weather. Rain in night and early morning.

Richard Jefferies, 1880 (Surrey)

APRIL

APRIL 1

Gossamer floats. Wood-larks hang suspended in the air, and sing all night.   *Gilbert White, 1776 (Hampshire)*

APRIL 2

Peaches and nectarines in bloom make a glorious show. Thomas began this day mowing the grass-walks.
Gilbert White, 1776 (Hampshire)

. . . Quite lovely spring day. All the working time in wood without greatcoat. Fullest gush of streams with the night's rain I ever saw. Now . . . lovely sleet showers with melting sunshine.   *John Ruskin, 1885 (Coniston Lake, Lancashire)*

APRIL 3

The *chif-chaf* . . . is heard in the Hanger, and Long Lythe. They are usually heard about the 21 of March. These birds, no bigger than a man's thumb, fetch an echo out of the hanger at every note.   *Gilbert White, 1791 (Hampshire)*

APRIL 4

A lovely sky as I walked out from British Museum, delicatest white agatescent cloud, helped me.
John Ruskin, 1876 (London)

APRIL 5

The air smells very sweet, and salubrious. Men dig their hop-gardens, and sow spring corn. . . . Dug some of the quarters in the garden, and sowed onions, parsnips, radishes and lettuces. Planted more beans in the meadow. Many flies are out basking in the sun.

Gilbert White, 1793 (Hampshire)

APRIL 6

Walked a short distance up the lesser Coombe, with an intention of going to the source of the brook, but the evening closing in, cold prevented us. The Spring still advancing very slowly. The horse-chestnuts budding, and the hedgerows beginning to look green, but nothing fully expanded. *Dorothy Wordsworth, 1798 (Somerset)*

Thunder. The cows getting with rough tongue into the sweet grass. . . . Arum, and blackbirds whistling. So beautiful, even the dust. *Richard Jefferies, 1880 (Surrey)*

APRIL 7

I note that on some trees—sycamore, chestnut, blackthorn —the lower buds open into leaf earlier than those on the upper branches. Mountain-ash, on the contrary, seems to spend its first energies upon its topmost shoots.

George Sturt, 1897 (Surrey)

APRIL 8

No birds sing, and no insects appear during this wintry, sharp season. *Gilbert White, 1770 (Hampshire)*

I rode yesterday out of the white atmosphere of Bath into the green village of Bath-Easton; and found myself by instinct at the *mill*, surrounded by weirs, backwaters, nets and willows, with a smell of weeds, flowing water, and flour in my nostrils. I need not say that the scene brought you [John Constable] to my mind, and produced this letter.

John Fisher, 1825 (Somerset)

APRIL 9

Walked to Stowey, a fine air in going, but very hot in returning. The sloe in blossom, the hawthorns green, the larches in the park changed from black to green in two or three days. *Dorothy Wordsworth, 1798 (Somerset)*

APRIL 10

Found a branch of white thorn in Porter's Snow, close-knotted and nearly in flower. *John Clare, 1825 (Northants)*

Tree pipit. The rolled ploughed field smooth like a lake. White butterfly. Willow wren.

Richard Jefferies, 1881 (Surrey)

APRIL 11

Swallow amidst frost and snow.

Gilbert White, 1770 (Hampshire)

Thames very full and beautiful, after so much dry weather: wheat looks well; meadows dry, and scorched; roads very dusty. *Gilbert White, 1790 (Oxford)*

Very cold, barren, growless weather still.

James Woodforde, 1796 (Norfolk)

APRIL 12

Walked in the morning in the wood. In the evening up the Coombe, fine walk. The Spring advances rapidly, multitudes of primroses, dog-violets, periwinkles, stitchwort.

Dorothy Wordsworth, 1798 (Somerset)

[Easter Sunday] This morning was bleak and most ungenial; a chilly sunshine, a piercing wind, a prevalence of watery cloud,—April weather, without the tenderness that ought to be half revealed in it.

Nathaniel Hawthorne, 1857 (York)

APRIL 13

(After tea) The air was become still, the lake was of a bright slate colour, the hills darkening. The bays shot into the low fading shores. Sheep resting. All things quiet.

Dorothy Wordsworth, 1802 (Westmorland)

APRIL 14

Lower part of the elms out and the chestnut fans rising into shape. *Gerard Manley Hopkins, 1869 (Surrey)*

The blossoming fruit trees, the torch trees of Paradise, blazed with a transparent green and white lustre up the dingle in the setting sunlight. The village is in a blaze of fruit blossom. *Francis Kilvert, 1872 (Radnorshire)*

APRIL 15

I heard the nightingale sing, but faintly. This evening I heard the young rooks. *Richard Hayes, 1762 (Kent)*

When we were in the woods beyond Gowbarrow park we saw a few daffodils close to the water-side. We fancied that the lake had floated the seeds ashore, and that the little colony had so sprung up. But as we went along there were more and yet more; and at last, under the boughs of the trees, we saw that there was a long belt of them along the shore, about the breadth of a country turnpike road. I never saw daffodils so beautiful. They grew among the mossy stones about and about them; some rested their heads upon these stones as on a pillow for weariness; and the rest tossed and reeled and danced, and seemed as if they were verily laughing with the wind, that blew upon them over the lake; they looked so gay, ever glancing, ever changing. This wind blew directly over the lake to them. There was here and there a little knot, and a few stragglers a few yards higher up; but they were so few as not to disturb the simplicity, unity, and life of that one busy highway.   *Dorothy Wordsworth, 1802 (Westmorland)*

[April 15th?] The half-opened wood-sorrel leaves, the centre or spring of the leaflets dropping back like ears leaving straight-chipped clefts between them, look like some green lettering and cut as sharp as dice.
                    Gerard Manley Hopkins, 1871 (Lancashire)

A bright hot sun and cold east wind, the sky a deep and wonderful blue and the roads dry. . . . The sun glared blinding upon the white flint road and the white chalkland, and the great yellow dandelions by the roadside stared at the sun.   *Francis Kilvert, 1874 (Wiltshire)*

APRIL 16

Green wood-pecker laughs at all the world. Storm-cock sings.   *Gilbert White, 1770 (Hampshire)*

The long bracken, unreapt, wet, and rotting, lying, strait dangling, from the mossy stone-hillocks like an unkempt red brown hair.   *S. T. Coleridge, 1802 (Cumberland)*

(Good Friday) When I undrew my curtains in the morning. I was much affected by the beauty of the prospect, and the change. The sun shone, the wind had passed away, the hills looked chearful, the river was very bright as it flowed into the lake. . . . After William had shaved we set forward. . . . A sheep came plunging through the river, stumbled up the bank, and passed close to us. . . . Its fleece dropped a glittering shower under its belly. Primroses by the road-side, pile wort that shone like stars of gold in the sun, violets, strawberries, retired and half-buried among the grass. . . . The view above Ambleside very beautiful. There we sate and looked down upon the green vale. We watched the crows at a little distance from us become white as silver as they flew in the sunshine, and when they went still further, they looked like shapes of water passing over the green fields.   *Dorothy Wordsworth, 1802 (Westmorland)*

APRIL 17

Hay is become very scarce and dear indeed! My rick is now almost as slender as the waist of a virgin; and it would have been much for the reputation of the last two brides that I have married, had their waists been as slender. . . . The first swallow that I heard of was on April 6th., the first nightingale April 13th. The great straddle-bob, Orion, that in the winter seems to bestride my brew-house, is seen now descending of an evening, on one side foremost behind the hanger.   *Gilbert White, 1786 (Hampshire)*

I saw a robin chasing a scarlet butterfly this morning.
     Dorothy Wordsworth, 1802 (Westmorland)

Saw a shoal of salmon in the river and many hares on the open hills. Under a stone hedge was a dying ram: there ran slowly from his nostril a thick flesh-coloured ooze, scarlet in places, coiling and roping its way down, so thick that it looked like fat. . . . Magnetic weather, sunlight soft and bright, colours of fells and fields far off seeming as if dipped in watery blue.

Gerard Manley Hopkins, 1873 (Lancashire)

APRIL 18

This morning I married John Knight and Elizabeth Austin at Langley Burrell Church. It was April weather with showers and gleams by whiles. . . . Rice and flowers were showered upon the bride in the porch and churchyard. There were three carriages with greys and postilions in scarlet. *Francis Kilvert, 1876 (Wiltshire)*

Yesterday there was deep snow, though the trees are in bloom. Plum trees and cherry trees full of blossom look so queer in a snow landscape, their lovely foamy fullness goes a sort of pinky drab, and the snow looks fiendish in its cold incandescence. I hated it violently.

D. H. Lawrence, 1918 (Berkshire)

APRIL 19

Up at 5, out at 6, in calm morning, wholly glorious. Lake like a dream. . . . Entirely Paradise of a day, cloudless and pure till 5: then East wind a little, but clearing for twilight. Did little but saunter among primroses and work on beach.

John Ruskin, 1873 (Coniston Lake, Lancashire)

Thermometer at 60. Wind S.W. Sky-Lark, Chaffinch, Thrush, Wren, and Robin singing. Horse-Chesnut, Wild-Bryar, Bramble and Sallow had spread their leaves. Blackthorn, double-flowered Peach, and Pears in full bloom; Double Jonquils, Hyacinths, Anemones, single Wall-flowers, and Auriculas in flower. In the fields, Dog-Violets, Daisies, Dandelion, Buttercups, Red-Archangel, and Shepherd's Purse.   *Thomas Gray, 1760 (Cambridgeshire)*

Young elmleaves lash and lip the sprays. This has been a very beautiful day—fields about us deep green lighted underneath with white daisies, yellower fresh green of leaves above which bathes the skirts of the elms, and their tops are touched and worded with leaf too. . . . Blue shadows fell all up the meadow at sunset and then standing at the far Park corner my eye was struck by such a sense of green in the tufts and pashes of grass, with purple shadow thrown back on the dry black mould behind them, as I do not remember ever to have been exceeded in looking at green grass.   *Gerard Manley Hopkins, 1874 (Surrey)*

To-day rosy dawn and woodsmoke: the most beautiful thing I ever saw in water reflection in all my life.
          John Ruskin, 1873 (Coniston Lake, Lancashire)

I was called up this morning before four o'clock. It was full light to dress myself: and so by water against tide, it being a little cool, to Greenwich; and thence, only that it was somewhat foggy till the sun got to some height, walked with great pleasure to Woolwich, in my way staying several times to listen to the nightingales.

Samuel Pepys, 1664 (Kent)

As we came down the lower slopes of the wooded hillside into the glade of the park the herds of deer were moving under the brown oaks and the brilliant green hawthorns.

Francis Kilvert, 1876 (Herefordshire)

APRIL 23

It being a beautiful morning we set off at 11 o'clock, intending to stay out of doors all the morning. . . . We determined to go under Nab Scar. . . . The sun shone and we were lazy. . . . It was very grand when we looked up, very stony, here and there a budding tree. . . . Looking into the vales,— Ambleside vale, with the copses, the village under the hill, and the green fields—Rydale, with a lake all alive and glittering, yet but little stirred by breezes, and our own dear Grasmere, first making a little round lake of nature's own, with never a house, never a green field, but the copses and the bare hills enclosing it, and the river flowing out of it. Above rose the Coniston Fells, in their own shape and colour—not Man's hills, but all for themselves, the sky and the clouds, and a few wild creatures.

Dorothy Wordsworth, 1802 (Westmorland)

Saw the redstart or firetail to-day and little willow wren. The blackthorn tree in full flower that shines about the hedges like cloaths hung out to dry.

John Clare, 1825 (Northants)

. . . to Croyland, over miserable peat flats in miserable grey storm, thundrous at once and biting cold, and as black as soot over Croyland bridge as I tried to draw.

John Ruskin, 1876 (Lincolnshire)

APRIL 24

Hail, stormy, strong wind. The wind broke off the great elm
in the churchyard short in two; the head of which injured
the yew tree. . . . Many tulips and other flowers are injured
by the hail.   *Gilbert White, 1779 (Hampshire)*

APRIL 25

The nightingale is now nearly in every bush.
                          Richard Hayes, 1764 (Kent)

The Ring-dove hangs on its wings, and toys in the air.
                          Gilbert White, 1777 (Hampshire)

. . . came slipping, sliding, scrambling down the precipitous
path of deep red mud, greasy with the rain. . . . In a field
adorned with a noble pear tree of majestic height and
growth in full blossom I found cowslips and the first bluebells and the young ferns uncurling their crozier heads.
                    Francis Kilvert, 1876 (Herefordshire)

APRIL 26

Beech spotted like a trout with the separate shadows of its
young leaves. . . . Leaf-strewn ground . . . beech mast under
beeches; beech leaves 9 inches deep drifted against felled
tree.   *Richard Jefferies, 1883 (Sussex)*

APRIL 27

Some hail, which made the evening very cold, a flash of
lightening, a clap of thunder, and a bright rainbow.
                    Gerard Manley Hopkins, 1868 (Hampstead)

I walked on over the Little Mountain to Gilfach yr heol.
The cross I cut on one of the silver birches near the Cayau
was nearly obliterated by the growth of the tree. I went up

to the hawthorn, 'the little lonely tree', on the brow of the Little Mountain. The cross there too was scarcely to be seen. I cut fresh crosses on the hawthorn and the silver birch. *Francis Kilvert, 1876 (Radnorshire)*

APRIL 28

Walnut showing leaf. Sycamore and Horsechestnut nearly cover'd. I observed a snail on his journey at full speed and I marked by my watch that he went 13 inches in 3 minutes, which was the utmost he could do without stopping to wind or rest. *John Clare, 1825 (Northants)*

APRIL 29

A beautiful morning—the sun shone and all was pleasant. . . . William lay, and I lay, in the trench under the fence— he with his eyes shut, and listening to the waterfalls and the birds. There was no one waterfall above another—it was a sound of waters in the air—the voice of the air. William heard me breathing and rustling now and then, but we both lay still, and unseen by one another; he thought that it would be as sweet thus to lie so in the grave, to hear the *peaceful* sounds of the earth, and just to know that our dear friends were near.
Dorothy Wordsworth, 1802 (Westmorland)

APRIL 30

The young rooks cried out from their nests lightly veiled in the fresh tender green of the elms around the Manor Farm. *Francis Kilvert, 1875 (Wiltshire)*

There is a wagtail sitting on the gate-post. I see how sweet and swift heaven is. But hell is slow and creeping and viscous and insect-teeming; as is this Europe now, this England. *D. H. Lawrence, 1915 (Sussex)*

MAY

MAY 1

To Westminster, in the way meeting many milkmaids with their garlands upon their pails, dancing with a fiddler before them.   *Samuel Pepys, 1665 (London)*

The grass crisp with white frost. Tulips hang their heads in the morning, being pricked with the frost.
                    Gilbert White, 1776 (Hampshire)

Sunday. . . . No service at church this morning, being under repair. A most gracious rain almost the whole night. Lord make us thankfull for the same. All vegetation seems at the height of growing.   *James Woodforde, 1796 (Norfolk)*

As soon as breakfast was over, we went into the garden, and sowed the scarlet beans about the house. It was a clear sky, a heavenly morning. I sowed the flowers, William helped me. We then went and sate in the orchard till dinner time. It was very hot. William wrote *The Celandine.*
                    Dorothy Wordsworth, 1802 (Westmorland)

We have a cherry tree from head to foot every branch sleeved with white glossy blossom.
                    Gerard Manley Hopkins, 1872 (Lancashire)

MAY 2

A bright cold morning, and while the sun was yet low the shadow of one of the five poplars fell across part of the spire of another, deepening and richening the green.
                    Francis Kilvert, 1870 (Radnorshire)

Lovely at last; dew in Rokeby parks, and sun on budding branches. Walked up Greta bed and found Brignal church-yard with my own Madonna herb all over the little chapel. Stayed long by the altar: at least, the place where it had been; Greta murmuring through the small east window. The little piscina uninjured. The woods all jewelled through with anemone and primrose, and perfect peace everywhere. *John Ruskin, 1876 (North Riding)*

MAY 3

Cold. Morning raw and wet, afternoon fine. . . . Cowslips capriciously colouring meadows in creamy drifts. Bluebells, purple orchis. Over the green water of the river passing the slums of the town and under its bridges swallows shooting, blue and purple above and shewing their amber-tinged breasts reflected in the water.

Gerard Manley Hopkins, 1866 (Oxford)

MAY 4

The brook and Painscastle mill pond glancing like silver. A beautiful sunny afternoon and the cuckoo calling every-where. *Francis Kilvert, 1870 (Radnorshire)*

MAY 5

Shot three greenfinches, which pull off the blossoms of the polyanths. *Gilbert White, 1784 (Hampshire)*

We walked in the twilight, and walked till night came on. The moon had the old moon in her arms, but not so plain to be seen as the night before. When we went to bed it was a boat without the circle.

Dorothy Wordsworth, 1802 (Westmorland)

MAY 6

By the backwardness of the spring my elm trees in the rookery are uncommon backward in putting out into leaf, so that there is little or no appearance of the buds putting forth. So that to all appearance the nests are as naked as though the depths of winter, notwithstanding we have taken young rooks for a fortnight past.

Richard Hayes, 1770 (Kent)

Great showers, and hail all round. Showers of hail at a distance look of a silvery colour. Rainbow. The hanger is bursting with leaf every hour. A progress in the foliage may be discerned every morning, and again every evening.

Gilbert White, 1786 (Hampshire)

A sweet morning. . . . The small birds are singing, lambs bleating, cuckow calling, the thrush sings by fits, Thomas Ashburner's axe is going quietly (without passion) in the orchard, hens are cackling, flies humming, the women talking together at their doors, plum and pear trees are in blossom—apple trees greenish.

Dorothy Wordsworth, 1820 (Westmorland)

First summer-feeling day. . . . The banks are 'versed' with primroses, partly scattered, partly in plots and squats, and at a little distance shewing milkwhite or silver—little spilt till-fulls of silver. I have seen them reflected in green standing farmyard water.

Gerard Manley Hopkins, 1871 (Lancashire)

MAY 7

The bloom of the fruit trees is the finest I ever saw in England. The pear-bloom is, at a distance, like that of the Guelder Rose; so large and bold are the bunches. The plum is equally fine; and even the blackthorn (which is the hedge-plum) has a bloom finer than I ever saw it have before. *William Cobbett, 1823 (Surrey)*

I see how chestnuts in bloom look like big seeded straw-berries. *Gerard Manley Hopkins, 1874 (Surrey)*

MAY 8

Green gooseberries. Lapwing's eggs at the poulterers.
Gilbert White, 1769 (Hampshire)

MAY 9

The turtles were trilling softly and deeply in the dingles as I went up the steep orchard. The grass was jewelled with cowslips and orchises. The dingle was lighted here and there with wild cherry, bird cherry, the Welsh name of which being interpreted is 'the tree on which the devil hung his mother'. The mountains burned blue in the hot afternoon. *Francis Kilvert, 1870 (Radnorshire)*

MAY 10

Nothing but cold east winds, accompanied with sunshine. . . . At the beginning of this month I saw fruit trees in blossom, stretched out flat against stone walls, reminding me of a dead bird nailed against the side of a barn. . . . The east-wind feels even rawer here than in the city [Liverpool].
Nathaniel Hawthorne, 1857 (Lancashire)

MAY 11

In the clough (the bluebells) came in falls of sky-colour washing the brows and slacks of the ground with vein-blue.
Gerard Manley Hopkins, 1871 (Lancashire)

This is the bitterest bleakest May I ever saw. . . . A black bitter wind violent and piercing drove from the east with showers of snow. The mountains and Clyro Hill and Cusop Hill were quite white with snow. The hawthorn bushes are white with may and snow at the same time.

Francis Kilvert, 1872 (Radnorshire)

Bluebells in Hodder wood, all hanging their heads one way. I caught as well as I could while my companions talked the Greek rightness of their beauty, the lovely—what people call—'gracious' bidding one to another or all one way, the level or stage or shire of colour they make hanging in the air a foot above the grass, and a notable glare the eye may abstract and sever from the blue colour—of light beating up from so many glassy heads, which like water is good to float their deeper instress in upon the mind.

Gerard Manley Hopkins, 1873 (Lancashire)

MAY 12

The rhubarb-tart good, and well flavoured.

Gilbert White, 1790 (Hampshire)

A real May-day at last; warm, west wind, sunshine; birds singing as if hearts would burst; four or five blackbirds all in hearing at once . . . song of thrush more varied even than nightingale; if rare, people would go miles to hear it, never the same in same bird, and every bird different; fearless, too.

Richard Jefferies, 1879 (Surrey)

MAY 13

Up before three o'clock, and a little after upon the water, it being very light as at noon, and a bright sun-rising; but by & by a rainbow appeared, the first that ever in a morning I saw.

Samuel Pepys, 1664 (London)

Cut the first bundle of asparagus.

Gilbert White, 1784 (Hampshire)

Ashen shoots injured by the late frosts, and kidney-beans and potato sprouts killed.

Gilbert White, 1791 (Hampshire)

MAY 14

A very cold morning—hail and snow showers all day . . . we . . . walked backwards and forwards in Brothers wood. William tired himself with seeking an epithet for the cuckoo. *Dorothy Wordsworth, 1802 (Westmorland)*

Lark singing beautifully in the still dark and clouded sky at a quarter to three o'clock in the morning; about twenty minutes afterwards the first thrush; thought I heard distant cuckoo—not sure; and ten minutes after that the copse by garden perfectly ringing with the music . . . southerly wind, warm light breeze, smart showers of warm rain, and intervals of brilliant sunshine; the leaves in copse beautiful delicate green, refreshed, cleaned, and a still more lovely green from the shower; behind them the blue sky, and above the bright sun; white detached clouds sailing past.

Richard Jefferies, 1879 (Surrey)

I find the country very beautiful. The apple trees are leaning forwards, all white with blossom, towards the green grass. I watch, in the morning when I wake up, a thrush on the wall outside the window—not a thrush, a blackbird— and he sings, opening his beak. It is a strange thing to watch his singing, opening his beak and giving out his calls and warblings, then remaining silent. He looks so remote, so buried in primeval silence, standing there on the wall, and bethinking himself, then opening his beak to make the strange, strong sounds. He seems as if his singing were a sort of talking to himself, or of thinking aloud his strongest thoughts. I wish I was a blackbird, like him. I hate men.

D. H. Lawrence, 1915 (Sussex)

MAY 15

Sheared my mongrel dog Rover, and made use of his white hair in plaster for ceilings. His coat weighed four ounces. The N.E. wind makes Rover shrink.

Gilbert White, 1788 (Hampshire)

MAY 16

Nightingales visit my fields and sing awhile: but withdraw, and travel on: some years they breed with me.

Gilbert White, 1778 (Hampshire)

Warm and mild, after a fine night of rain. Transplanted radishes after breakfast . . . gathered mosses and plants. . . . All flowers now are gay and deliciously sweet. The primrose still pre-eminent among the later flowers of the spring. Foxgloves very tall, with their heads budding. . . . Grasmere very solemn in the last glimpse of twilight.

Dorothy Wordsworth, 1800 (Westmorland)

I had a very comfortable journey. The country in the bright morning light was simply bowed down with beauty —heavy, weighed down with treasure. Shelley's moonlight may glittered everywhere. . . . I have never seen anything more solemn and splendid than England in May—and I have never seen a spring with less of the *jeune fille* in it.

Katherine Mansfield, 1918 (After train journey from Paddington to Cornwall)

Incessant rain from morning till night. . . . The Skobby [chaffinch] sat quietly in its nest, rocked by the wind, and beaten by the rain.

Dorothy Wordsworth, 1800 (Westmorland)

. . . to Combe Wood to see and gather bluebells, which we did, but fell in bluehanded with a gamekeeper, which is a humbling thing to do. Then we heard a nightingale utter a few strains—strings of very liquid gurgles.

Gerard Manley Hopkins, 1874 (Surrey)

Farringford. Walked with Tennyson among the trees and lawns. Tennyson said, 'White lilac used to be my favourite flower.' *William Allingham, 1866 (Isle of Wight)*

Went with Dora at 3 o'clock to a picnic in the Marsh. . . . We played hide-and-seek in the wood and danced Sir Roger de Coverley under the oaks in the green glade near the keeper's lodge. Agnes and Edith made a pretty picture once for a moment as they stood together on the mound at the foot of one of the oaks, dressed alike sisterly in bright magenta skirts.

The sheets of bluebells were still in all their splendour and the pink rhododendrons were just beginning to show their blossoms. *Francis Kilvert, 1874 (Wiltshire)*

Great Bear at $\frac{1}{2}$ to 8 to 9 exactly *at zenith*. The Rider precisely overhead. *Richard Jefferies, 1880 (Surrey)*

Do you know what guelder roses are? Big sumptuous white clusters with a green light upon them. We must grow them.

Katherine Mansfield, 1918 (Cornwall)

MAY 19

Black-cap sings sweetly, but rather inwardly.
Gilbert White, 1770 (Hampshire)

MAY 20

A fine mild rain. After breakfast the sky cleared and before the clouds passed from the hills I went to Ambleside.
It was a sweet morning. Everything green and overflowing
with life, and the streams making a perpetual song, with
the thrushes and all little birds, not forgetting the stone-
chats.　　　　　*Dorothy Wordsworth, 1800 (Westmorland)*

Whitsunday. . . . Beautiful blackness and definition of elm
tree branches in evening light (from behind). Cuckoos calling and answering to each other, and the calls being not
equally timed they overlapped, making the triple *cuckoo*,
and crossed.　　　*Gerard Manley Hopkins, 1866 (Berkshire)*

MAY 21

A mockery of bright sunshine day after day, no rain . . .
wind always holding from the north, dim blue skies, faint
clouds, ashy frosts in the mornings: saw young ivy leaves
along the sunk fence bitten and blackened.
Gerard Manley Hopkins, 1874 (Surrey)

MAY 22

My [Horse] Chesnutt walk (in front of my house) is now
out in full leaf and show their long blooming stem for
blowing.　　　　　　　*Richard Hayes, 1770 (Kent)*

63

Took Annie to look for crab-blossom, but grieved to find anemones all gone; oxalis also destroyed by frost and wind. Primroses buried in grass, but the hyacinths coming.

John Ruskin, 1886 (Coniston, Lancashire)

Ground parched. Then a thunderstorm, and after that the nightingales singing at night.

Gerard Manley Hopkins, 1874 (Surrey)

MAY 23

This spring has been very different from last: so dry and bright: no rain for weeks, always sunshine and dryness: no fog. . . . The gorse is out in masses this year, and the blackthorn a great white smoke.

D. H. Lawrence, 1917 (Cornwall)

MAY 24

Swifts copulate in the air, as they flie.

Gilbert White, 1785 (Hampshire)

The country is simply wonderful, blue, graceful little companies of bluebells everywhere on the moors, the gorse in flame, and on the cliffs and by the sea, a host of primroses, like settling butterflies, and seapinks like a hover of pink bees, near the water. There is a Spanish ship run on the rocks just below—great excitement everywhere.

D. H. Lawrence, 1916 (Cornwall)

MAY 25

The martins have just finished the shell of a nest left unfinished in some former year under the eaves of my stable.

Gilbert White, 1774 (Hampshire)

MAY 26

Much gossamer. The air is full of floating cotton from the willows. *Gilbert White, 1786 (Hampshire)*

Do not like cloudless skies so much as the clouds tramping on one behind the other. The cloudless sky does not look so large. The sparkles on the water—like butterflies flapping their wings. *Richard Jefferies, 1881 (Surrey)*

MAY 27

The fens of Lincolnshire—green, green, and nothing else. *Nathaniel Hawthorne, 1857*

. . . banks and hedges brilliant with pink campion. . . . As I came home the western heavens were jewelled with pure bright sparkling lights of grey silver and pale gold, and overhead a sublime mackerel sky of white and blue in its distant fleecy beauty gave me a more intense and grand sense of infinity and the illimitable than I ever remember to have had before. *Francis Kilvert, 1874 (Wiltshire)*

My bedroom is illuminated all day with a beautiful rosy light from the glorious blossom of the pink may on the lawn. *Francis Kilvert, 1875 (Wiltshire)*

MAY 28

The Flycatcher, which was not seen till the 18th., has got a nest, and four eggs. *Gilbert White, 1788 (Hampshire)*

My weeding-woman swept up on the grass-plot a bushel basket of blossoms from the white apple-tree: and yet that tree seems still covered with bloom.
Gilbert White, 1793 (Hampshire)

We sate in the orchard. The sky cloudy, the air sweet and cool. The young bullfinches, in their party-coloured raiment, bustle about among the blossoms, and poize themselves like wire-dancers or tumblers, shaking the twigs and dashing off the blossoms. There is yet one primrose in the orchard. The stitchwort is fading. The wild columbines are coming into beauty, the vetches are in abundance, blossoming and seeding. . . . In the garden we have lilies, and many other flowers. The scarlet beans are up in crowds. It is now between 8 and nine o'clock. It has rained sweetly for two hours and a half; the air is very mild. The heckberry blossoms are dropping off fast, almost gone—barberries are in beauty—snowballs coming forward—May roses blossoming.

Dorothy Wordsworth, 1802 (Westmorland)

MAY 29

With my wife and the two maids and the boy took boat and to Vauxhall, where I had not been a great while. To the old Spring Garden, and there walked long, and the wenches gathered pinks.   *Samuel Pepys, 1662 (Surrey)*

The grass under my windows is all bespangled with dewdrops, and the birds are singing in the apple trees, among the blossoms. Never poet had a more commodious oratory in which to invoke his Muse.

William Cowper, 1786 (Buckinghamshire)

MAY 30

Walking to Marnhull. The prime of bird-singing. The thrushes and blackbirds are the most prominent,—pleading earnestly rather than singing, and with such modulation that you seem to see their little tongues curl inside their bills in their emphasis. A bullfinch sings from a tree with a metallic sweetness piercing as a fife. Further on I come to a hideous carcase of à house in a green landscape, like a skull on a table of dessert.

Thomas Hardy, 1877 (Dorset)

MAY 31

Grass grows very fast. Honey-suckles very fragrant, and most beautiful objects! Columbines make a figure. My white thorn, which hangs over the earth-house, is now one sheet of bloom, and has pendulous boughs down to the ground. *Gilbert White, 1792 (Dorset)*

We sat out all day.
Dorothy Wordsworth, 1802 (Westmorland)

Walk in the garden at midnight and hear corncrake.
William Allingham, 1865 (Donegal)

JUNE

JUNE 1

Sainfoin is large, and thick, and lodged [beaten down] by
the rain.   *Gilbert White, 1770 (Hampshire)*

Potted nine tall balsams, and put the pots in a sunk bed.
Dragon-flies have been out some days. The oaks in many
places are infested with caterpillars . . . to such a degree as
to be quite naked of leaves. These palmer-worms hang
down from the trees by long threads.
                          Gilbert White, 1786 (Hampshire)

Men wash their fatting sheep; and bay the streams to catch
trouts. Trouts come up our shallow streams almost to the
spring-heads to lay their spawn.
                          Gilbert White, 1791 (Hampshire)

On the top of the Downs a whole fire of gorse.
                          D. H. Lawrence, 1915 (Sussex)

JUNE 2

Walked about by moonlight in the evening. Wondered
what woman, if any, I should be thinking about in five
years' time.   *Thomas Hardy, 1865 (London)*

JUNE 3

Wind S.S.E. Thermometer at 84 (the highest I ever saw it):
it was at Noon. Since which till last week we had hot dry
weather. Now it rains like mad. Cherries and Strawberries
in bushels.   *Thomas Gray, 1760 (Cambridgeshire)*

[Sending flowers with a letter] I *love* the yellow rock-roses:
but they are so frail, I wonder if you'll ever see them as they
really are. I'm afraid they'll be all withered. They are pure
flowers of light—and they cover the dry, limey hills . . . the
yellow pansies . . . grow sprinkled close all over the tiny
meadow just under the house, and so glittery standing on
the close turf—like a Fra Angelico meadow.

D. H. Lawrence, 1918 (Derbyshire)

JUNE 4

I brought home lemon thyme, and several other plants,
and planted them by moonlight.

Dorothy Wordsworth, 1800 (Westmorland)

JUNE 5

My brother Thomas White nailed up several large scallop
shells under the eaves of his house at South Lambeth, to
see if the house-martins would build in them. These con-
veniences had not been fixed up half an hour before several
pairs settled upon them; and expressing great complacency,
began to build immediately.

Gilbert White, 1782 (Hampshire)

JUNE 6

Everything grows, if tempests would let it; but I have had
two of my largest trees broke to-day with the wind.

Horace Walpole, 1752 (Middlesex)

Slate quarries, one great pillar left standing; ship under the
cliff loading; dived into a cavern all polished with the
waves like dark marble with veins of pink and white.

Follow'd up a little stream falling thro' the worn slate, smoked a pipe at little inn, dined, walked once more to the old castle [Tintagel] darkening in the gloom.

Alfred Tennyson, 1848 (Cornwall)

JUNE 7

Tulips are faded. Honeysuckles still in beauty. My columbines are very beautiful. Tied some of the stems with pieces of worsted, to mark them for seed. Planted out pots of green cucumbers.   *Gilbert White, 1783 (Hampshire)*

Another glowing glorious day of sunshine and unclouded blue. But every day the drought grows drier and the predicted water famine is stealing upon us. Every day the pasture grows whiter and more bare and slippery. . . . Later the warm soft night was laden with perfume and the sweet scent of the syringa.   *Francis Kilvert, 1874 (Wiltshire)*

JUNE 8

The trout leaping in the sunshine spreads on the bottom of the river concentric circles of light.

S. T. Coleridge, 1802 (Cumberland)

Walked seaward. Large crimson clover; sea purple and green like a peacock's neck. 'By bays, the peacock's neck in hue.'   *Alfred Tennyson, 1848 (Cornwall)*

JUNE 9

A soaking all day rain. . . . The hawthorns on the mountain sides like orchards in blossom.

Dorothy Wordsworth, 1802 (Westmorland)

Everything seemed parched and dried up by the two months' drought except some brilliant patches of crimson sainfoin which lighted up the white hot downs and burning Plain.   *Francis Kilvert, 1874 (Wiltshire)*

It is now the time of long days, when the sun seems reluctant to take leave of the trees at evening—the shine climbing up the trunks, reappearing higher, and still fondly grasping the tree-tops till long after.
Thomas Hardy, 1917 (Dorset)

JUNE 10

Eleven at night. I am just come out of the garden in the most oriental of evenings, and from breathing odours beyond those of Araby. The acacias, which the Arabians have the sense to worship, are covered with blossoms, the honeysuckles dangle from every tree in festoons, the seringas are thickets of sweets, and the new-cut hay in the fields tempers the balmy gales with simple freshness; while a thousand sky-rockets launched into the air at Ranelagh or Marybone illuminate the scene, and give it an air of Haroun Alraschid's paradise.
Horace Walpole, 1765 (Middlesex)

To Brockenhurst . . . croquet, roses, hot sun. Field path to station, red campions and kingcups.
William Allingham, 1867 (Hampshire)

JUNE 11

We have had an extraordinary drought, no grass, no leaves, no flowers; not a white rose for the festival of yesterday! About four arrived such a flood, that we could not see out of the windows: the whole lawn was a lake, though situated

on so high an Ararat. . . . You never saw such desolation.
. . . It never came into my head before, that a rainbow-
office for insuring against water might be very necessary.

Horace Walpole, 1775 (Middlesex)

Elder begins to blow. When the elder blows out the summer
is at its height.   *Gilbert White, 1773 (Hampshire)*

JUNE 12

Male glow-worms, attracted by the light of the candles,
come into the parlour. The distant hills look very blue.

Gilbert White, 1791 (Hampshire)

JUNE 13

The fogs . . . still continue, though till yesterday the earth
was as dry as intense heat could make it. The sun continues
to rise and set without his rays, and hardly shines at noon.
At eleven last night the moon was a dull red; she was nearly
at her highest elevation, and had the colour of heated
brick. . . . Dead ducks cannot travel this weather; they say
it is too hot for them, and they shall stink. ·

William Cowper, 1783 (Buckinghamshire)

In the evening we walked. . . . It was a silent night. The
stars were out by ones and twos, but no cuckow, no little
birds, the air was not warm. . . . We walked to our new
view of Rydale, but it put on a sullen face. There was an
owl hooting in Bainriggs. Its first halloo was so like a
human shout that I was surprized, when it made its second
call tremulous and lengthened out, to find the shout had
come from an owl. The full moon (not quite full) was
among a company of steady island clouds, and the sky
bluer about it than the natural sky blue.

Dorothy Wordsworth, 1802 (Westmorland)

The parsley fern grew in sheets of brilliant green among the grey shale.

Francis Kilvert, 1871 (Cader Idris, Merioneth)

JUNE 14

We had just the skirts of a vast thunder-storm.

Gilbert White, 1775 (Hampshire)

It froze hard last night: I went out for a moment to look at my haymakers, and was starved. The contents of an English June are hay and ice, orange-flowers and rheumatism. I am now cowering over the fire.

Horace Walpole, 1791 (Middlesex)

I had the bud of a purple flagflower in water and happening to touch it it broke open.

Gerard Manley Hopkins, 1872 (Lancashire)

JUNE 15

Rode all day with some trouble, for fear of being out of our way, over the Downs, where the life of the shepherds is, in fair weather only, pretty. In the afternoon come to Avebury, where, seeing great stones like those of Stonehenge standing up, I stopped and took a countryman of that town, and he carried me and showed me a place trenched in like Old Sarum almost, with great stones pitched in it, some bigger than those of Stonehenge in figure, to my great admiration. *Samuel Pepys, 1668 (Wiltshire)*

The sun and the golden buttercup meadows had it almost to themselves. . . . One or two people were crossing the Common early by the several paths through the golden sea

of buttercups which will soon be the silver sea of ox-eyes.
The birds were singing quietly. The cuckoo's notes tolled
clear and sweet as a silver bell.

Francis Kilvert, 1873 (Wiltshire)

William and I went to Brathey by Little Langdale and
Collath and Skelleth. It was a warm mild morning with
threatening of rain. The vale of Little Langdale looked
bare and unlovely. Collath was wild and interesting, from
the peat carts and peat gatherers—the valley all perfumed
with the Gale [bog myrtle] and wild thyme. The woods
about the waterfall veined with rich yellow broom.

Dorothy Wordsworth, 1800 (Westmorland)

I looked at the pigeons down in the kitchen yard and so on.
They look like little gay jugs by shape when they walk,
strutting and jod-jodding with their heads. The two
young ones are all white and the pins of the folded wings,
quill pleated over quill, are like crisp and shapely cuttle-
shells found on the shore. The others are dull thunder-
colour or black-grape-colour except in the white pieings,
the quills and tail, and in the shot of the neck. I saw one up
on the eaves of the roof: as it moved its head a crush of
satin green came and went, a wet or soft flaming of the
light.
    Sometimes I hear the cuckoo with wonderful clear and
plump and fluty notes: it is when the hollow of a rising
ground conceives them and palms them up and throws
them out, like blowing into a big humming ewer.

Gerard Manley Hopkins, 1873 (Lancashire)

Gleams of sunshine on rain and poppies.

John Ruskin, 1875 (Oxfordshire)

The weather has changed: it's really more lovely than ever, but showery—immense clapping showers of rain, castles and mountains in the sky and reflected in the purple sea, the air smelling of elder flower and seaweed.

Katherine Mansfield, 1918 (Cornwall)

JUNE 17

We had a full view of the balloon—which looked so near that I could see the divisions of colored silk. On its rising higher we saw it on a clear blue sky looking like a golden egg—it then went into a thin white cloud—and then emerged from it with great beauty, one side so very bright —and the other so clear and dark. Looked till it was hidden by other clouds. *John Constable, 1824 (London)*

JUNE 18

A hollow place in the rock like a coffin—a sycamore bush at the head, enough to give a shadow for my face, and just at the foot one tall foxglove—exactly my own length— there I lay and slept. It was quite soft.

S. T. Coleridge, 1801 (Westmorland)

Grey all day; no sunshine, except for a quarter of an hour on the roses, leaving Thame. All wet with rain they were and infinitely lovely. *John Ruskin, 1875 (Oxfordshire)*

JUNE 19

Very cold indeed again to-day, so cold that Mrs. Custance came walking in her spencer with a bosom-friend.[1]

James Woodforde, 1799 (Norfolk)

[1] Mrs. Custance, as a lady of fashion, would have worn her gowns low cut, in the bosomy manner so often drawn by Rowlandson: in cold weather she would have needed the fashionable item of clothing known as the 'bosom-friend'.

Set off for Polperro, ripple-mark, queer old narrow-streeted place, back at 9. Turf fires on the hills; jewel-fires in the waves from the oar, which Cornish people call 'bryming'.

Alfred Tennyson, 1848 (Cornwall)

Two beautiful anvil clouds low on the earthline in opposite quarters, so that I stood between them.

Gerard Manley Hopkins, 1871 (Lancashire)

Foxgloves now everywhere between the rocks and ferns.

D. H. Lawrence, 1916 (Cornwall)[1]

JUNE 20

The elders, water-elders wild guelder roses, foxgloves, and other solstitial plants begin to be in bloom. Blue dragon-flies appear.

Gilbert White, 1778 (Hampshire)

We lay upon the sloping turf. Earth and sky were so lovely that they melted our very hearts. The sky to the north was of a chastened yet rich yellow, fading into pale blue, and streaked and scattered over with steady islands of purple, melting away into shades of pink. It made my heart almost feel like a vision to me.

Dorothy Wordsworth, 1802 (Westmorland)

JUNE 21

We have now frosty mornings, and so cold a wind, that even at high noon we have been obliged to break off our walk in the southern side of the garden, and seek shelter, I in the greenhouse, and Mrs Unwin by the fireside. Hay-making begins here to-morrow.

William Cowper, 1784 (Buckinghamshire)

[1] See also June 27.

Put sticks to some of the kidney-beans. Longest day: a cold harsh solstice! The rats have carried away six out of seven of my biggest bantam chickens; some from the stable, and some from the brew-house.

Gilbert White, 1792 (Hampshire)

What is the matter with to-day? It is thin, white, as lace curtains are white, full of ugly noises. . . . Went for a walk and was caught in the wind and rain. Terribly cold and wretched. . . .   *Katherine Mansfield, 1918 (Cornwall)*

JUNE 22

Fruit-walls in the sun are so hot that I cannot bear my hand on them. Brother Thomas's thermometer was 89 on an east wall in the afternoon. Much damage was done, and some persons killed by lightning on this sultry day.

Gilbert White, 1790 (Hampshire)

I never saw the elder bushes so filled with blossom—they are quite beautiful—and some of their blossom forshortened as they curve over the round head of the tree itself are quite elegant—it is a favourite of mine and always was—but 'tis melancholy.   *John Constable, 1835 (Hampstead)*

JUNE 23

I walked in the afternoon to Shorne windmill. Saw St Paul's, London. With my glass and naked eye I could discern it.   *Richard Hayes, 1771 (Kent)*

The meadows have been parched to a January brown, and we have foddered our cattle for some time, as in the winter.

William Cowper, 1788 (Buckinghamshire)

I walked to the top of the hill and sate under a wall near John's Grove, facing the sun. I read a scene or two in *As You Like It*. . . . A sullen, coldish evening, no sunshine; but . . . a light came out suddenly that repaid us for all. It fell only upon one hill, and the island [in Grasmere], but it arrayed the grass and trees in gem-like brightness.

Dorothy Wordsworth, 1802 (Westmorland)

Sea evenings dark, short, soon dark after sundown; no lingering light and colour and softness as inland among orchards and meadows.   *Richard Jefferies, 1884 (Sussex)*

JUNE 24

Thunder, and hail. A sad midsummer day.

Gilbert White, 1792 (Hampshire)

Swifts squeak much. The swifts that dash round churches, and towers in little parties, squeaking as they go, seem to me to be the cock-birds: they never squeak til they come close to the walls or eaves, and possibly then are serenading their females, who are close in their nests attending to the business of incubation. Swifts keep out the latest of any birds, never going to roost in the longest days til about a quarter before nine. Just before they retire they squeak and dash and shoot with wonderful rapidity. They are stirring at least seventeen hours when the days are longest.

Gilbert White, 1774 (Hampshire)

The custom is in this part of Hertfordshire . . . to leave a *border* around the ploughed part of the fields to bear grass and to make hay from, so that, the grass being now made into hay, every corn field has a closely mowed grass walk about ten feet wide all round it, between the corn and the hedge. This is most beautiful! The hedges are now full of the shepherd's rose, honeysuckles, and all sorts of wild

81

flowers; so that you are upon a grass walk, with this most beautiful of all flower gardens and shrubberies on your one hand, and with the corn on the other. And thus you go from field to field (on foot or on horseback), the sort of corn, the sort of underwood and timber, the shape and size of the fields, the height of the hedge-rows, the height of the trees, all continually varying. Talk of *pleasure-grounds* indeed! What, that man ever invented, under the name of pleasure-grounds, can equal these fields in Hertfordshire.

William Cobbett, 1822

Camps of yellow flagflower blowing in the wind, which curled over the grey sashes of the long leaves.

Gerard Manley Hopkins, 1873 (Lancashire)

JUNE 25

I write in a nook that I call my *Boudoir*. It is a summer-house not much bigger than a sedan chair, the door of which opens into the garden, that is now crowded with pinks, roses, and honeysuckles, and the window into my neighbour's orchard. . . . Having lined it with garden mats, and furnished it with a table and two chairs, here I write all that I write in summer-time, whether to my friends, or to the public.   *William Cowper, 1785 (Buckinghamshire)*

JUNE 26

The moon rose large and dull like an ill-cleaned brass plate, slowly surmounts the haze, and sends over the calm sea a faint bright pillar.

Dorothy Wordsworth, 1828 (Isle of Man)

JUNE 27

Met a cart of whortle-berries on the road.
                                   Gilbert White, 1788 (Hampshire)

(27th?) Always, when I see foxgloves, I think of the Lawrences.[1] Again I pass in front of their cottage, and in the
window—between the daffodil curtains with the green
spots—there are the great, sumptuous blooms.

  'And how beautiful they are against whitewash!' cry
the Lawrences.

  As is their custom, when they love anything, they make
a sort of Festa. With foxgloves everywhere. And then they
sit in the middle of them like blissful prisoners, dining in
an encampment of Indian Braves.
                           Katherine Mansfield, 1918 (Cornwall)

JUNE 28

Put on a half shirt first this summer, it being very hot, and
yet so ill-tempered am I grown, that I am afeard I shall
catch cold, while all the world is ready to melt away.
                                   Samuel Pepys, 1664 (London)

In the evening walked sadly along the shore of the Solent,
eastwards by Pylewell . . . returning, brought home a glow-
worm and put it in a white lily, through which it shone.
                           William Allingham, 1863 (Hampshire)

Across stepping stones of Tees in twilight, feeling there
was life in me yet. Stood long on the single arch of the
bridge, looking at the deep river and glen.
                              John Ruskin, 1867 (North Riding)

[1] D. H. Lawrence and Frieda Lawrence, at Zennor. *See also June 19.*

Clouded morning, a little rain, afterwards fine. . . . The rustling of the green corn and the play of various tints now light, now darker green as the breeze rushes over it. . . . Moon S.W. ½ full, west, Venus low down. Sky palest blue, stars faint, shimmering—whitish wheat rustling: Aspens rustling in dark copse, white flint heaps; white road: cool S.W. breeze.   *Richard Jefferies, 1879 (Surrey)*

JUNE 29

Young minute frogs migrate from the ponds this showery weather, and fill the lanes and paths: they are quite black.
                    Gilbert White, 1775 (Hampshire)

Called at Hay Castle and went with the four pretty girl archers to shoot and pick up their arrows in the field opposite the Castle.   *Francis Kilvert, 1872 (Breconshire)*

JUNE 30

I climbed to the top of the walls [of Tintern Abbey] and looked down into the vast square deep well formed by the four great lofty arches of nave, choir and transepts which upheld the great central tower of the Church. The top of the walls was adorned with a perfect wild-flower garden of scarlet poppies, white roses, yellow stonecrop and purple mallows, which formed a low hedge along each side of the otherwise undefended footpath or thickness of the walls, and which climbed with profuse luxuriance over the ruins of the summit of the walls. From this perch, on a level with the jackdaws . . ., I looked down into the green-floored enclosure of the grey ruins and into the streets of the village where the people looked dreadfully small as they moved about the roads and garden paths.
                Francis Kilvert, 1875 (Monmouthshire)

JULY

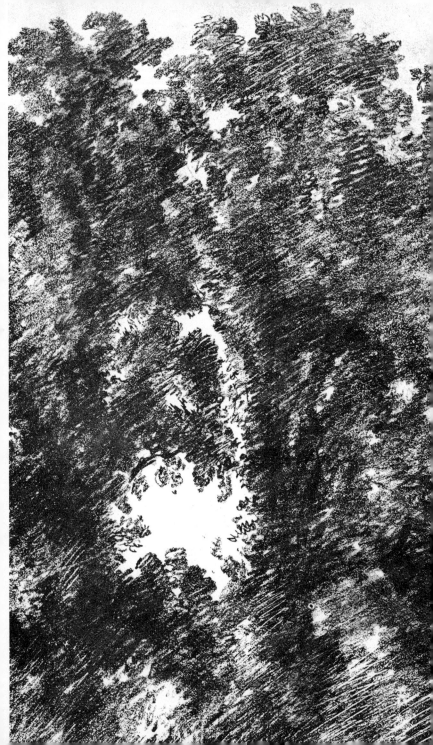

JULY 1

Out in the morning first thing studying wild roses.
John Ruskin, 1884 (Coniston, Lancashire)

JULY 2

Low creeping mists. Yellow evening.
Gilbert White, 1784 (Hampshire)

A very rainy morning. There was a gleam of fair weather, and we thought of walking into Easedale. Molly began to prepare the linen for putting out, but it rained worse than ever.   *Dorothy Wordsworth, 1802 (Westmorland)*

JULY 3

I shiver with cold on this present third of July. . . . Last Saturday night the cold was so severe that it pinched off many of the young shoots of our peach-trees. . . . The very walnuts, which are now no bigger than small hazelnuts, drop to the ground; and the flowers, though they blow, seem to have lost their odours. I walked with your mother yesterday in the garden, wrapped up in a winter surcoat, and found myself not at all encumbered by it.
William Cowper, 1782 (Buckinghamshire)

Hops do not cover their poles well, checked perhaps by the cold, black weather.   *Gilbert White, 1773 (Hampshire)*

Cold and rain and very dark. I was sick and ill. . . . William walked out a little, I did not. We sate at the window together. It came on a terribly wet night. Wm. finished *The Leech Gatherer.*

Dorothy Wordsworth, 1802 (Westmorland)

When I went out, after breakfast, there were gleams of sunshine here and there on the hillsides, falling one did not exactly see how, through the volumes of cloud. . . . I rather think this particular stretch of Loch Lomond, in front of Inversnaid, is the most beautiful lake and mountain view that I have ever seen. It is so shut in that you can see nothing beyond, nor would suspect anything more to exist than this watery vale among the hills. . . . The mists, this morning, had a very soft and beautiful effect, and made the mountains tenderer than I have hitherto felt them to be; and they lingered about their heads like morning-dreams flitting and retiring, and letting the sunshine in, and snatching it away again. My wife came up, and we enjoyed it together, till the steamer came smoking its pipe along the loch, stopped to land some passengers, and steamed away again.   *Nathaniel Hawthorne, 1857 (Stirlingshire)*

Dull, showery, and cold. . . . Tea-coloured shoots on the roses and pink-purple shaded into green. Gliding and winding of white-poplar sprays in the wind.

Gerard Manley Hopkins, 1866 (Hampstead)

A very sweet morning. William stayed some time in the orchard. . . . It came on a heavy rain, and we could not go to Dove Nest as we had intended. . . . The roses in the garden are fretted and battered and quite spoiled, the honey suckle, though in its glory, is sadly teazed. The peas are beaten down. The scarlet beans want sticking. The garden is overrun with weeds.

Dorothy Wordsworth, 1802 (Westmorland)

JULY 6

Phallus impudicus olet.[1] Young daws come forth. Cut my Sainfoin: a vast crop. Vast showers about.

Gilbert White, 1770 (Hampshire)

Went to Land's End by Logan rock, leaden-backed mews wailing on cliff, one with two young ones. Mist. Great yellow flare just before sunset. Funeral. Land's End and Life's End. *Alfred Tennyson, 1848 (Cornwall)*

Netley Abbey . . . a most picturesque and perfect ruin, all ivy-grown, of course, and with great trees where the pillars of the nave used to stand, and also in the refectory and the cloister court; and so much soil on the summit of the broken walls, that weeds flourish abundantly there, and grass too; and there was a wild rose-bush, in full bloom, as much as thirty or forty feet from the ground.

Nathaniel Hawthorne, 1856 (Hampshire)

JULY 7

In the morning William nailed up the trees while I was ironing. We lay sweetly in the orchard. . . . The orchard full of foxgloves. The honeysuckle beautiful—plenty of roses, but they are battered. . . . Walked on the White Moss. Glow-worms. Well for them children are in bed when they shine. *Dorothy Wordsworth, 1802 (Westmorland)*

[1] *Phallus impudicus* (i.e. the Stinkhorn fungus) *smells.*

Rain, rain, rain. Bees cluster round the mouth of one hive; but cannot swarm. . . . The young swallows that come out are shivering, and ready to starve.

Gilbert White, 1777 (Hampshire)

The Lizard, rocks in sea, two southern eyes[1] of England. Tamarisk hedge in flower. Round Pentreath beach, large cranesbill near Kynance, down to cove. Glorious grass-green monsters of waves. Into caves of Asparagus Island. Sat watching wave-rainbows.

Alfred Tennyson, 1848 (Cornwall)

After much rain, some thunder, and no summer as yet, the river swollen and golden . . . there was this day a thunder-storm on a greater scale—huge rocky clouds lit with livid light, hail and rain that flooded the garden, and thunder ringing and echoing round like brass.

Gerard Manley Hopkins, 1871 (Lancashire)

April storms. Shower and shine chasing each other swiftly. . . . The red roses in the garden bright against the sunny light blue mountains.   *Francis Kilvert, 1871 (Radnorshire)*

Heat has come on now. The air is full of the sweet acid of the limes. The trees themselves are starrily tasselled with the blossom.   *Gerard Manley Hopkins, 1874 (Surrey)*

Fine. Distances in shades of blue, but quite without haze. . . . The wheat-fields blue underneath, but now warm green in the ear.   *Gerard Manley Hopkins, 1866 (Hampstead)*

[1] i.e. the two Lizard lighthouses.

JULY II

Destroyed a wasp's nest which was grown into a considerable bulk, and had many working wasps.

Gilbert White, 1775 (Hampshire)

JULY 12

Vine bloom smells sweetly.

Gilbert White, 1771 (Hampshire)

Much struck . . . in coming from London by the lovely. green of everything; certainly England gains more by summer or rather loses more in winter than any country I have seen in both seasons.

John Ruskin, 1847 (Warwickshire)

I noticed the smell of the big cedar, not just in passing it but always at a patch of sunlight on the walk a little way off. I found the bark smelt in the sun and not in the shade and I fancied too this held even of the smell it shed in the air.   *Gerard Manley Hopkins, 1874 (Surrey)*

JULY 13

Mighty hot weather, I lying this night, which I have not done, I believe, since a boy, with only a rug and sheet upon me.   *Samuel Pepys, 1667 (London)*

Bathed in Polpur Cove. Bewick-like look of trunk, cloak and carpet bag, lying on rock. Sailed, could not land at Kynance. Saw the long green swell heaving on the black cliff.   *Alfred Tennyson, 1848 (Cornwall)*

I found a strange fish on the shore with rainbows about its wild staring eyes, enclosed in a sort of sack with long tentacula beautifully coloured, quite dead, but when I took it up by the tail it spotted all the sand underneath with great drops of ink, so I suppose it was a kind of cuttle-fish. I found too a pale pink orchis on the sea bank. . . .

Alfred Tennyson, 1852 (North Riding)

JULY 14

. . . in the cool of the evening all the way. . . . We had the pleasure to see several glow-worms which was mighty pretty.

Samuel Pepys, 1667 (Surrey, between Epsom and London)

A heavy shower came on, but we buttoned ourselves up both together in the Guard's coat, and we liked the hills and the rain the better for bringing us so close to one another. . . . At last however it grew so very rainy that I was obliged to go into the coach at Bowes. . . . I was right glad to get out again to my own dear brother at Greta Bridge; the sun shone chearfully, and a glorious ride we had over Gaterly Moor. Every building was bathed in golden light. The trees were more bright than earthly trees, and we saw round us miles beyond miles.

Dorothy Wordsworth, 1802 (North Riding)

JULY 15

Made jellies, and jams of red currants. Gathered broad beans. . . . The cat gets upon the roof of the house, and catches young bats as they come forth from behind the sheet of lead at the bottom of the chimney.

Gilbert White, 1786 (Hampshire)

Arrived very hungry at Rievaulx . . . at an exquisitely neat farmhouse we got some boiled milk and bread; this strengthened us, and I went down to look at the ruins. Thrushes were singing, cattle feeding among green-grown hillocks about the ruins. These hillocks were scattered over with *grovelets* of wild roses and other shrubs, and covered with wild flowers. I could have stayed in this solemn quiet spot till evening, without a thought of moving, but William was waiting for me, so in a quarter of an hour I went away.
Dorothy Wordsworth, 1802 (North Riding)

Seen in Midsummer, 15 July 9 o'clock P.M. At that time of twilight when the azure behind a high spired turret was very cool but almost blueless, the chastened glow of the light tower against it was very beautiful the sky being textureless and without a cloud, but what I write this for is to remark that though all was low in tone as preparing to receive the still and solemn night, yet the tower on which the last light glimmered, seemed luminous in itself and rather sending out light from itself than reflecting it, and I noticed it on other stone buildings going along that it was as if they had inherent light somewhat reminding one of mother-of-pearl—it was luminous though pale, faint and glimmering.   *Samuel Palmer, 1824 (Kent?)*

We entered Mark Ash, a wood of huge solemn beech trees, the floor thick-matted with dead leaves; a few trees were broken or fallen; some towered to a great height before branching. We sat on the roots of a mighty beech. T[ennyson] smoked. We shared in sandwiches and brandy. Then he produced a little pocket *As You Like It*, and read some parts aloud.   *William Allingham, 1866 (New Forest)*

JULY 16

A wonderful dark sky and shower of rain this morning. At Harwich a shower of hail as big as walnuts.

Samuel Pepys, 1666 (Essex)

As I walked along the field path I stopped to listen to the rustle and solemn night whisper of the wheat, so different to its voice by day. *Francis Kilvert, 1873 (Wiltshire)*

JULY 17

The jasmine is so sweet that I am obliged to quit my chamber. *Gilbert White, 1783 (Hampshire)*

JULY 18

Showers and fine; rainbow.—The reason Shakespeare calls it 'the blue bow'—to put it down now precisely—is because the blue band edged by and ending in violet, though not the broadest, is the deepest expression of colour in the bow and so becomes the most decisive and emphatic feature there.—At sunset the air rinsed after the rain.

Gerard Manley Hopkins, 1867 (Hampstead)

JULY 19

Those oaks that were stripped by caterpillars begin to be cloathed with verdure. Many beeches are loaded with mast, so that their boughs become very pendulous, and look brown. *Gilbert White, 1786 (Hampshire)*

Intensely hot day—left off a waistcoat, and for yarn wore silk stockings. *S. T. Coleridge, 1803 (Cumberland)*

JULY 20

Much thunder. Some people in the village were struck
down by the storm, but not hurt. The stroke seemed to
them like a violent push or shove. The ground is well
soaked. Wheat much lodged [laid flat].

Gilbert White, 1778 (Hampshire)

JULY 21

The planet Mars figures every evening and makes a golden
and splendid shew. This planet being in opposition to the
sun, is now near us, and consequently bright.

Gilbert White, 1781 (Hampshire)

On the beach at Hunstanton. The sun a round plate of
red gold dipping near the Sea among lilac-gray clouds—
the Sea itself steel colour with a touch of yellow in it. Due
north it is grand to think there is nothing between yourself and the ice-bergs. . . . (N.B.—Always spell 'Sea' with a
capital S, it is only right.) The feet make no sound on the
flat wide sands. You hear the sound of your pencil as you
write. All human beings have become distant black dots.

James Smetham, 1870 (Norfolk)

JULY 22

A huge hornet. T[ennyson]kills it.

William Allingham, 1866 (Hampshire)

. . . we got into the serpentine district. The roads were
made of marble, black marble, the dust of which looked
like coal dust. The country became very wild and timber
almost disappeared. Along the roadsides grew large bushes
of beautiful heather, white, pink and rose colour, growing

freely as gorse grows with us. We stopped the carriage and gathered some fine sprays. The splendour and luxuriance of the heather, I never saw anything like this before. . . . At last we got off and drove to Kynance Cove. . . . The tide was ebbing fast and it was nearly low water. We wandered about through the Dining Room and Drawing Room caves, and through the huge serpentine cliffs and the vast detached rocks which stand like giants guarding the Cove. I never saw anything like the wonderful colour of the serpentine rocks, rich, deep, warm, variegated, mottled and streaked and veined with red, green and white, huge blocks and masses of precious stone marble on every side, an enchanted cove, the palace of the Nereids.

Francis Kilvert, 1870 (Cornwall, the Lizard)

To-day the heat was excessive and as I sat reading under the lime I pitied the poor haymakers toiling in the burning Common where it seemed to be raining fire.

Francis Kilvert, 1873 (Wiltshire)

Hot sun, little crackling sounds among the wheat, increasing as the wind blew. *Richard Jefferies, 1884 (Sussex)*

JULY 23

To Beaumont. . . . It was a lovely day: shires-long of pearled *cloud under cloud*, with a grey stroke underneath marking each row; beautiful blushing yellow in the straw of the uncut ryefields, the wheat looking white and all the ears making a delicate and very true crisping along the top and with just enough air stirring for them to come and go gently; then there were fields reaping.

Gerard Manley Hopkins, 1874 (Surrey to Berkshire)

JULY 24

Robert says the first grass from the scythe is the *swathe*, then comes the *strow* (tedding), then *rowing*, then the foot-cocks, then *breaking*, then the *hubrows*, which are gathered into *hubs*, then sometimes another break and *turning*, then *rickles*, the biggest of all the cocks, which are run together into *placks*, the shapeless heap from which the hay is carted. *Gerard Manley Hopkins, 1871 (Lancashire)*

JULY 25

The water shines in the fallows.
Gilbert White, 1778 (Hampshire)

We drank tea to-night before I left Grasmere, on the island in that lovely lake; our kettle swung over the fire, hanging from the branch of a fir-tree, and I lay and saw the woods, and mountains, and lake all trembling, and as it were idealized through the subtle smoke, which rose up from the clear, red embers of the fir-apples which we had col-lected: afterwards we made a glorious bonfire on the margin, by some elder-bushes, whose twigs heaved and sobbed in the uprushing column of smoke, and the image of the bonfire, and of us that danced round it, ruddy, laughing faces in the twilight; the image of this in a lake, smooth as that sea to whose waves the Son of God had said *Peace!* *S. T. Coleridge, 1800 (Westmorland)*

JULY 26

It rained almost incessantly at Keswick till the late evening, when it fell a deep calm, and even the leaves, and very top-most leaves, of the poplars and aspens had holiday, and like an overworked boy consumed it in sound sleep. . . . The clouds were scattered by wind and rain in all shapes and heights, above the mountains, on their sides, and low down to their bases—some masses in the middle of the valley—when the wind and rain dropt down and died, and for two hours all the clouds, white and fleecy all of them, remained without motion, forming an appearance not very unlike the moon as seen thro' a telescope. . . . Blessings on the Mountains! to the eye and ear they are always faithful. I have often thought of writing a set of play-bills for the Vale of Keswick—for every day in the year—announcing each day the performance, by his supreme Majesty's Servants, Clouds, Waters, Sun, Moon, Stars, etc.

S. T. Coleridge, 1802 (Cumberland)

Breakfast in Paris—so to train. Across in intensely calm water and sky. The smoke of steamers on clear cliffs of England in a streak all round horizon. . . . I never saw the cliffs themselves so clearly from France.

John Ruskin, 1872 (English Channel)

JULY 27

Tortoise eats gooseberries.

Gilbert White, 1780 (Hampshire)

Very warm. . . . John bathed in the lake [Grasmere]. . . . After tea we rowed down to Loughrigg Fell, visited the white foxglove, gathered wild strawberries, and walked up to view Rydale. We lay a long time looking at the lake; the shores all embrowned with the scorching sun. The ferns were turning yellow, that is, here and there one was quite turned.   *Dorothy Wordsworth, 1800 (Westmorland)*

JULY 28

The showers do not at all moisten the ground, which remains as hard as iron.   *Gilbert White, 1769 (Hampshire)*

JULY 29

Elms at end of twilight are very interesting: against the sky
they make crisp scattered pinches of soot.
Gerard Manley Hopkins, 1867 (Hampstead)

Torrents of lashing and streaming rain all the morning, a
thunderstorm without thunder breaking into a beautiful
sunny afternoon. I went to Hay to pay some bills. On the
crest of the hill above Hay I met a tall woman smoking a
clay pipe and driving a black donkey.
Francis Kilvert, 1871 (Radnorshire–Breconshire)

JULY 30

Peacocks begin to moult and cast their splendid train. Total
eclipse of the moon.   *Gilbert White, 1776 (Hampshire)*

Total eclipse of the moon. Came on soon after 10 in the
evening. Began on the left side of the moon, and in about
one hour was totally eclipsed, so that all her beautiful
glittering (borrowed) light was quite gone; but not so far
gone that you might not discern her. She appeared of a
beautiful orange colour like (not near so red as) blood,
resembling the light she appears in through a fog. Total
darkness said to continue till about three quarters after
one. But I went to bed soon after she was totally eclipsed.
Richard Hayes, 1776 (Kent)

There was much most beautiful in the fresh level meadows
on each side of the road; and a little divergence from it,
once, brought me to the side of the Avon, a noiseless, yet
not lazy stream, lying like the inlet of a lake between
shadowy groups and lines of elm and aspen, quiet and
something sad. A group of cattle, very young and very
gentle, lying on a little promontory of cool grass in the

shade, and yet so brown and bright white that they looked like sunshine, and lay as quietly, the water-lilies resting like them in their own place—their bud-like poppy-seed fruit, poised in the deep water—(note, this fruit all full of yellow seeds, enclosed in a woolly receptacle)—and a fair, far-reaching sky, all full of white clouds like endless marble stairs, descending over the tall trees of Warwick park.

I was struck, as I walked back, by the starry groups of plantain with a little mixed clover, edging the footpath, covered with dust so as to take off its green. The plaintain seeds standing up, gave it relief; it might have been turned into bronze on the instant, and put Ghiberti to shame.

John Ruskin, 1847 (Warwickshire)

JULY 31

The ground is dried to powder.

Gilbert White, 1772 (Hampshire)

Gathered peas, and in the afternoon Coleridge came, very hot. . . . The men went to bathe, and we afterwards sailed down to Loughrigg. Read poems on the water, and let the boat take its own course. . . . The moon just setting as we reached home.

Dorothy Wordsworth, 1800 (Grasmere, Westmorland)

We mounted the Dover Coach at Charing Cross. It was a beautiful morning. The city, St Paul's, with the river and a multitude of little boats, made a most beautiful sight as we crossed Westminster Bridge. The houses were not over-hung by their cloud of smoke, and they were spread out endlessly, yet the sun shone so brightly, with such a fierce light, that there was even something like the purity of one of nature's own grand spectacles.

Dorothy Wordsworth, 1802 (London)

AUGUST

A large ball of fire (about 11 at night) was seen to fall on Shorne windmill during the thunder tempest. The explosion blow'd the weather boarding off for several rods of the mill, took the top swip off, and down the main post and shivered it much.   *Richard Hayes, 1776 (Kent)*

The poor begin to glean wheat. The country looks very rich, being finely diversified with crops of corn of various sorts, and colours.   *Gilbert White, 1786 (Hampshire)*

Very lovely with calm lake, but the roses fading, the hay cut. The summer is ended. Autumn begun.
          John Ruskin, 1884 (Coniston Lake, Lancashire)

AUGUST 2

The Fair. Gentry very doubtful of the weather. Never saw so few people pass. No ladies in their long carriages and the fewest horse people remembered.
          Richard Hayes, 1773 (Kent)

About eight o'clock it gathered for rain, and I had the scatterings of a shower, but afterwards the lake became of a glassy calmness, and all was still. I sate till I could see no longer.   *Dorothy Wordsworth, 1800 (Westmorland)*

I have been trying remedies for the hooping-cough, and have, I believe, tried everything, except riding, wet to the skin, two or three hours amongst the clouds on the South Downs. This remedy is now under trial. . . .

William Cobbett, 1823 (Sussex)

We have lived a few days on the seashore, with the waves banging up at us. Also over the river, beyond the ferry, there is the flat silvery world, as in the beginning, untouched: with pale sand, and very much white foam, row after row, coming from under the sky, in the silver evening: and no people, no people at all, no houses, no buildings, only a haystack on the edge of the shingle, and an old black mill. For the rest, the flat unfinished world running with foam and noise and silvery light, and a few gulls swinging like a half-born thought. It is a great thing to realise that the original world is still there—perfectly clean and pure, many white advancing foams, and only the gulls swinging between the sky and the shore; and in the wind the yellow sea poppies fluttering very hard, like yellow gleams in the wind, and the windy flourish of the seed-horns.

D. H. Lawrence, 1915 (Sussex)

AUGUST 3

Our meadows are covered with a winter-flood in August; the rushes with which our bottomless chairs were to have been bottomed, and much hay which was not carried, are gone down the river on a voyage to Ely, and it is even uncertain whether they will ever return. *Sic transit gloria mundi!*

William Cowper, 1782 (Buckinghamshire)

Somewhat of a chilly feel begins to prevail in the mornings and evenings. . . . Men house hay as black as old thatch.

Gilbert White, 1791 (Hampshire)

AUGUST 4

Rain in the night. I tied up scarlet beans, nailed the honey-suckles, etc. etc. . . . I pulled a large basket of peas. . . . A very cold evening.

Dorothy Wordsworth, 1800 (Westmorland)

Pass thro' Gosforth . . . leave the great road and go up by the Irt, thro' a stony road, behind me a beautiful view of the sea and the low-lands on the shore seen in that most impressive of all ways, viz, thro' an inverted arch formed by the rough fells before me, the huge enormous mountains of Wasdale all bare and iron-red—and on them a *forest* of cloud-shadows, all motionless. . . . Mem. beautiful shadow of the Fern upon the lichened stone which it overcanopied.

S. T. Coleridge, 1802 (Cumberland)

Half hour after sunset, pearl grey light west with scarlet. South, moon reddish yellow, bright, nearly full over palest amber wheat. Cloud of midges round hat. . . . Heavy shadows hung in foliage of the elms, silence except the sound of the reaper the other side of the hedge, slash, rustle-slash, rustle.

Richard Jefferies, 1884 (Kent)

AUGUST 5

Up Snae Fell. . . . You can see from it three kingdoms. The day was bright; pied skies. On the way back we saw eight or perhaps ten hawks together.

Gerard Manley Hopkins, 1873 (Isle of Man)

AUGUST 6

Unusually bright. From Jeffrey Hill . . . in the ridge opposite with Parlock Pike the folds and gullies with shadow in them were as sharp as the pleats in a new napkin and we made out in the sea, appearing as clearly outlined flakes of blue, the Welsh coast, Anglesea, and Man, and between these two the sea was as bright as brass.

Gerard Manley Hopkins, 1871 (Lancashire)

AUGUST 7

I got a boy at Selborne to show me along the lanes out into Woolmer forest on my way to Headley. The lanes were very deep; the wet *malme* just about the colour of rye-meal mixed up with water, and just about as clammy, came in many places very nearly up to my horse's belly.

William Cobbett, 1823 (Hampshire)

It rained hard while I staid in the cottage, but had ceased when I went over and out, and presently appeared such a bright far off streaky sky in the west seen over the glistening hedges as made my heart leap again . . . and the sun came out presently and every shake of the trees shoke down more light upon the grass; and so I came to the village, and stood leaning on the churchyard gate, looking at the sheep, nibbling and resting among the graves (newly watered they lay, like a field of precious seed). . . .

John Ruskin, 1847 (Warwickshire)

We went mackerel fishing. Letting down a line baited with a piece of mackerel skin—tin or any glimmering thing will do—we drew up nine. A few feet down they look like blue silver as they rise.

Gerard Manley Hopkins, 1872 (Isle of Man)

AUGUST 8

Pretty farmyard—thatch casting sharp shadow on white-wash in the sun, and a village rising beyond, all in a comb; sharp showers, bright clouds; sea striped with purple.

Gerard Manley Hopkins, 1877 (Devon)

AUGUST 9

A yellow sun fast setting, and all entwined with other in-
fluence, with the pale gibbous moon, with the scent of
honeysuckle.   *James Smetham, 1868 (Sussex)*

AUGUST 10

St Lawrence's Day. Meteor Day. . . . To-night was the great
August meteor shower and Uncle Will and I went up to
the gate to watch for the meteors which the Irish call
'St Lawrence's tears'.   *Francis Kilvert, 1871 (Wiltshire)*

It is pretty to see the dance and swagging of the light green
tongues or ripples of waves in a place locked between rocks.
                    Gerard Manley Hopkins, 1872 (Isle of Man)

Studied dew on Sweet William . . . the divine crimson
lighted by the fire of each minute lens.
                    John Ruskin, 1880 (Coniston Lake, Lancashire)

AUGUST 11

In a field among the woods the flax sheaves stood in shocks
like wheat, the fine-hung bells on their wiry hair stalks
rustling and quaking in the breeze like wag wantons.[1] A
mare and foal stood in the shade among the flax sheaves.
                    Francis Kilvert, 1871 (Dorset)

AUGUST 12

August, I hope, will make us amends for the gloom of its
many wintry predecessors. We are now gathering from our

[1] Quaking Grass.

meadows, not hay, but muck; such stuff as deserves not the carriage, which yet it must have, that the after-crop may have leave to grow. The Ouse has hardly deigned to run in his channel since the summer began.

William Cowper, 1789 (Buckinghamshire)

The planters think these foggy mornings, and sunny days, injurious to their hops.

Gilbert White, 1789 (Hampshire)

AUGUST 13

Entirely calm and clear morning. The mist from the river at rest among the trees, with rosy light on its folds of blue; and I, for the first time these ten years, happy.

John Ruskin, 1872 (Berkshire)

AUGUST 14

Sun and wind. . . . On the cliffs fields of bleached grass, the same colour as the sheep they feed, then a sleeve of liquid barley-field, then another slip of bleached grass, above that fleshy blue sky. Nearer at hand you see barley breathe and open and shut and take two colours and swim.

Gerard Manley Hopkins, 1873 (Isle of Man)

AUGUST 15

Took this morning by birdlime on the tips of hazel-twigs several hundred wasps that were devouring the gooseberries. A little attention this way makes vast riddance.

Gilbert White, 1783 (Hampshire)

The last gathering of wood-strawberries. Bullfinches and red-breasts eat the berries of the honeysuckles.

Gilbert White, 1790 (Hampshire)

AUGUST 16

Colchicums, or Naked Boys appear.
Gilbert White, 1791 (Hampshire)

I can hardly write for looking at the silvery clouds; how I sigh for that peace (to paint them) which this world cannot give, (to me at least). *John Constable, 1833 (Hampstead)*

Looking over my kitchen garden . . . I found it one miserable mass of weeds gone to seed; the roses in the higher garden putrified into brown sponges, feeling like dead snails; and the half-ripe strawberries all rotten at the stalks.
John Ruskin, 1879 (Coniston Lake, Lancashire)

AUGUST 17

The sun shone hot and bright down into the little valley among the hills, upon the wild white marsh cotton and the purple heather and the bright green Osmunda ferns with their brown flower spikes, and upon the white shirt sleeves of the peat cutters working among the mawn pits on a distant part of the Common . . . the mountains and the valley were glowing blue and golden in the evening sunlight. Above Pen y llan a crowd of purple thistles stood in fatal and mischievous splendour among the waving oats.
Francis Kilvert, 1872 (Radnorshire)

AUGUST 18

We sat on the down above Babbicombe bay. The sea was like blue silk. It seemed warped over towards our feet. Half-miles of catspaw like breathing on glass just turned the smoothness here and there. Red cliffs, white ashy shingle, green inshore water, blue above that, clouds and distant cliffs dropping soft white beams down it, bigger clouds making big white tufts of white broken by ripples of the darker blue foreground water as if they were great white roses sunk in a blue dye.

Gerard Manley Hopkins, 1874 (Devonshire)

AUGUST 19

Misty—dry early: later rain, evening heavy rain. Limes turning yellow and leaves falling: horsechestnuts too a little. *Richard Jefferies, 1879 (Surrey)*

AUGUST 20

This morning . . . intensely beautiful, pure blue seen through openings in quiet cloud and lake calm; but the clouds not quite right—tawny and too thick . . . chopping wood. Fairly fine with sweet air.

John Ruskin, 1875 (Coniston Lake, Lancashire)

AUGUST 21

Walked with John round the two lakes [Grasmere and Rydal Water]—gathered white foxglove seeds.

Dorothy Wordsworth, 1800 (Westmorland)

[At the Falls of Clyde] See the shapes below me, in 3 yards of water: smooth water in a vault, smooth water close to the smooth rock—a hollow, unquiet, and changeful between the waters. Water with glassy wrinkles, water with a thousand wrinkles all lengthways, water all puckered and all over dimples, over smooth rock rough with tiny roughnesses, the boiling foam below this fall.

S. T. Coleridge, 1803 (Lanarkshire)

Found glacier-marked stone in wood.

John Ruskin, 1875 (Coniston, Lancashire)

Very cold. Baking in the morning, gathered pea seeds and took up—lighted a fire upstairs. . . . Wind very high shaking the corn.   *Dorothy Wordsworth, 1800 (Westmorland)*

Dunbar. . . . It began to rain and remained black till sunset. George came down to tell me there was a rainbow on the sea. I ran up, and the noble column of fire was standing on the horizon, like the Israelites' pillar, the sea coming dark across its base, yet that sea still a pale grey neutral green, with white foam breaking it, the sky within the rainbow pale brick red, outside darker. As I stood marvelling at it, I was startled by what I thought at first was a meteor behind the rainbow, a spark of vivid fire in the midst of its colour. It was a seagull between me and it, that had got into the sun. Two or three others followed, and each, as it turned its wings to the sunshine, flamed like a star—perfect *feux follets* of rose colour. This was altogether new to me.

John Ruskin, 1847 (East Lothian)

AUGUST 23

Martins and swallows congregate by hundreds on the church and tower. These birds never cluster in this manner, but on sunny days. They are chiefly the first broods, rejected by their dams, who are busyed with a second family.

Gilbert White, 1785 (Hampshire)

I have been, in the dusk of the evening, taking a walk along Pevensey Level—a quiet, broad, seaside road; the wind soft and cool; the sky orange, most soft in the west, but with leaden, purple, ragged clouds floating here and there in masses and wild flakes about the sky, and dragging streaks of rain across the darkening downs. In the east, a large, rose-coloured, steadfast cloud arising from fresh

blue-gray banks of sinking nimbi, with the summer lightning incessantly fluttering in its bosom, like thoughts.

James Smetham, 1855 (Sussex)

Rain steady all morning: heavy till afternoon—caused
local flood. Evening dry but cloudy. The wood pigeons are
now in the wheat in flocks (they beat the ears with bill).

Richard Jefferies, 1879 (Surrey)

AUGUST 24

Sunday evening, walked to Latterrigg with Sara and Hart-
ley—the sun set with slant columns of misty light, slanted
from him: the light a bright buff—Walla Crag purple red,
the lake Derwentwater a deep dingy purple blue—that
Torrent Crag . . . a maroon. But the clouds . . . a fine *smoke-
flame.* . . . As we turned round on our return, we see a
moving pillar of clouds, flame and smoke, rising, bending,
arching, and in swift motion—from what God's chimney
doth it issue?—I scarcely ever saw in the sky such variety
of shapes, and colors, and colors floating over colors.—
Solemnly now lie the black masses on the blue firmament
of—not quite night—for still at the foot of Bassenthwaite
there is a smoky russet light.

S. T. Coleridge, 1800 (Cumberland)

AUGUST 25

Tintagel. Black cliffs and caves and storm and wind, but I
weather it out and take my ten miles a day walks in my
weather-proofs.   *Alfred Tennyson, 1860 (Cornwall)*

Late in the evening we loitered down into the water meads.
The sun was setting in stormy splendour behind Salisbury
and the marvellous aerial spire rose against the yellow glare

like Ithuriel's spear, while the last gleams of the sunset flamed down the long lines of the water carriages making them shine and glow like canals of molten gold.

Francis Kilvert, 1875 (Wiltshire)

AUGUST 26

Timothy the tortoise, who has spent the last two months amidst the umbrageous forests of the asparagus-beds, begins now to be sensible of the chilly autumnal mornings; and therefore suns himself under the laurel-hedge, into which he retires at night. He is become sluggish, and does not seem to take any food.   *Gilbert White, 1787 (Hampshire)*

AUGUST 27

It is so cold this 27th. of August that I shake in the greenhouse where I am writing.

William Cowper, 1782 (Buckinghamshire)

Morning—six o'clock—Clouds in motion half down Skiddaw, capping and veiling Wanthwaite. No sun, no absolute gleam, but the mountains in and beyond Borrodale were bright and *washed*—and the vale of Newlands silent, and bright. All the crags that enbason the Derwent Water very dark—especially Walla Crag, the crag such a very gloomy purple, its treeage such a very black green. . . . N.B. What is it that makes the silent *bright* of the morning vale so different from that other silence and bright gleams of late evening? Is it in the mind or is there any physical cause? . . .

8 o'clock—White cloud rolling along on the edge of a green sun-spot on the Bassenthwaite extremity of Skiddaw.

—½ 8. In this whole bason from the mountains of Borrodale to the hill behind Ouse Bridge but one field is sunny—

that with a white cottage—The grass yellow green, so bright —the white cottage sparkles like a diamond in the surrounding gloom.   *S. T. Coleridge, 1800 (Cumberland)*

I live almost wholly in the fields, and see nobody but the harvest men.   *John Constable, 1815 (Suffolk)*

AUGUST 28

[Five a.m.] A very fine morning. . . . My horse is ready; and the rooks have just gone off to the stubble-fields. These rooks rob the pigs; but they have *a right* to do it. I wonder (upon my soul I do) that there is no lawyer, Scotchman, or Parson-Judge, to propose a law to punish the rooks for *trespass.*   *William Cobbett, 1826 (Wiltshire)*

Rain in morning—has now rained 36 hours. All day yesterday, all night, and as hard as ever this morning, and continued till 2, when cleared after 36 hours rain. Then strong wind. . . . White bryony vines dying, berries red. Arum berries red (first) on stalk.   *Richard Jefferies, 1879 (Surrey)*

AUGUST 29

Home by starlight and Jupiter, stumbling down steep dark lanes.   *Gerard Manley Hopkins, 1867 (Devonshire)*

Opposite is Snowdon and its range, just now it being bright visible but coming and going with the weather. . . . The garden is all heights, terraces, Excelsiors, misty mountain tops, seats up trees called Crows' Nests, flights of steps seemingly up to heaven lined with burning aspiration upon aspiration of scarlet geraniums.
          Gerard Manley Hopkins, 1874 (Denbighshire)

Michaelmas daisy begins to blow.

Gilbert White, 1772 (Hampshire)

Wheat *bronzed*—light balls of thistledown rolling over it, the tips of the bronzed ears bending to that delicate touch. . . . Some birch trees—yellow leaves.

Richard Jefferies, 1879 (Surrey)

AUGUST 31

A great deal of corn is cut in the vale, and the whole prospect, though not tinged with a general autumnal yellow, yet softened down into a mellowness of colouring, which seems to impart softness to the forms of hills and mountains. At 11 o'clock Coleridge came, when I was walking in the still clear moonshine in the garden. He came over Helvellyn. William was gone to bed, and John also, worn out with his ride round Coniston. We sate and chatted till ½-past three. Coleridge read us a part of *Christabel.*

Dorothy Wordsworth, 1800 (Westmorland)

SEPTEMBER

✤❋✤

SEPTEMBER 1

The beards of thistle and dandelions flying above the lonely mountains like life, and I saw them thro' the trees skimming the lake like swallows.

S. T. Coleridge, 1800 (Grasmere, Westmorland)

From Tenterden I set off at five o'clock, and got to Appledore after a most delightful ride, the high land upon my right, and the low land upon my left. The fog was so thick and white along some of the low land, that I should have taken it for water, if little hills and trees had not risen up through it here and there.   *William Cobbett, 1823 (Kent)*

The chill, rainy English twilight brooding over the lawn.
Nathaniel Hawthorne, 1853 (Cheshire)

SEPTEMBER 2

. . . Entered Glencoe, the white mists (white, with interspaces of diluted black) floating away from the mountains, and thinning off along their breasts—gathering again—again thinning—all in motion—giving phantoms of motion even to the hills thro' the openings and rents of the mists—O those other rich white mists seen thro' the thinning of the nearer mist! and blue sky, here and there, in the *low* Heaven!   *S. T. Coleridge, 1803 (Argyll)*

119

Walked towards Shakespeare's Cliff; the fleet still in view. Looked down from the edge of the cliffs on the fine red gravel margin of the sea. Many vessels on the horizon and in mid-channel. The French coast, white and high, and clear in the evening gleam. Evening upon the sea becoming melancholy, silent and pale. A leaden-coloured vapour rising upon the horizon, without confounding the line of separation; the ocean whiter, till the last deep twilight falls, when all is one gradual, inseparable, undistinguishable, grey.   *Ann Radcliffe, 1797 (Sussex)*

Noon. Very sultry, with large drops of rain falling on my palette. Light air from S.W.
      John Constable (note on a drawing), ?1821 (Hampstead)

SEPTEMBER 4

Wood-owls hoot much.

                        Gilbert White, 1774 (Hampshire)

SEPTEMBER 5

The day was lovely and I went over to Newchurch. . . . A solitary fern cutter was at work on the Vicar's Hill mowing the fern with a sharp harsh ripping sound. In the first Newchurch field the turkeys, black and grey and fawn-coloured, were mourning in the stubbles and a black pony was gazing pensively over the hedge. I passed through two fields of thin stunted wheat almost choked with sow thistle which covered me with its downy blossom. From the Little Mountain the view was superb and the air exquisitely clear. The Clee Hills seemed marvellously near. The land glittered, variegated with colours and gleams of wheat, stubble and blue hill.   *Francis Kilvert, 1871 (Radnorshire)*

Rosy sea—sunset at Worthing.
Richard Jefferies, 1883 (Sussex)

SEPTEMBER 6

The morning suddenly became glorious and we saw what had happened in the night. All night long millions of gossamer spiders had been spinning and the whole country was covered. . . . The gossamer webs gleamed and twinkled into crimson and gold and green, like the most exquisite shot-silk dress in the finest texture of gauzy silver wire. I never saw anything like it or anything so exquisite as 'the Virgin's webs' glowed with changing opal lights and glanced with all the colours of the rainbow. At 4 o'clock Miss Meredith Brown and her beautiful sister Etty came over to afternoon tea with us and a game of croquet.
Francis Kilvert, 1875 (Wiltshire)

SEPTEMBER 7

In the dusk of the evening when beetles begin to buzz, partridges begin to call; these two circumstances are exactly coincident.   *Gilbert White, 1775 (Hampshire)*

SEPTEMBER 8

Peacock butterflies flitting over the sea of blue scabious, swinging, opening and shutting their broad wings and spreading their peacock eyes on the slope to the morning sun. Light fleecy clouds drifted along half way down the great slopes of the dim blue misty mountains.
Francis Kilvert, 1871 (Radnorshire)

The full moon at night in a palecoloured heartsease made of clouds.   *Gerard Manley Hopkins, 1873 (Surrey)*

Red-breasts whistle agreeably on the tops of hop-poles, etc.,
but are prognostic of autumn.

Gilbert White, 1781 (Hampshire)

. . . went straight up a field till I came to Barrow Gill—it
runs thro' a bed of rock. . . . Beautiful pools and water-
slides in this Gill . . . passed a moss peat, and beheld a
narrow bottom and on the other side a hill how high I
cannot see for the cloud. Grass and ling, most magnifi-
cently *streamed* with purple and scarlet screes.

S. T. Coleridge, 1800 (Cumberland)

SEPTEMBER 10

The swallows are flocking together in the skies ready for
departing and a crowd has dropt to rest on the walnut tree
where they twitter as if they were telling their young stories
of their long journey to cheer and check fears.

John Clare, 1824 (Northants)

A lovely autumn morning with a bright silvery mist on the
river [the Wye]. I walked to Hay over Llowes Common and
down through the cherry orchard and the pear orchard in
greater love than tongue can tell and beauty inexpressible.

Francis Kilvert, 1878 (Herefordshire–Breconshire)

SEPTEMBER 11

Red even, sweet moon. Some nightly thief stole a dozen of
my finest nectarines. *Gilbert White, 1791 (Hampshire)*

Between Somerford and Oaksey I saw, on the side of the
road, more goldfinches than I had ever seen together; I
think fifty times as many as I had ever seen at one time in

my life. The favourite food of the goldfinch is the seed of the thistle. This seed is just now dead ripe. The thistles are all cut and carried away from the fields by the harvest; but they grow alongside the roads; and, in this place, in great quantities. So that the goldfinches were got here in flocks, and as they continued to fly along before me for nearly half a mile, and still sticking to the road and the banks, I do believe I had, at least, a flock of ten thousand flying before me. *William Cobbett, 1826 (Wiltshire)*

SEPTEMBER 12

Cut my thumb. Walked in the fir-grove before dinner—after dinner sate under the trees in the orchard—a rainy morning, but very fine afternoon. . . . The fern of the mountains now spreads yellow veins among the trees; the coppice wood turns brown.
Dorothy Wordsworth, 1800 (Westmorland)

SEPTEMBER 13

I went down to my oast house at about 4 this morning (thick fog). I heard my hop dryer (William Mace) sing very melodious several psalm tunes. *Richard Hayes, 1772 (Kent)*

This morning was most beautiful. . . . As I came along I saw one of the prettiest sights in the flower way that I ever saw in my life. It was a little orchard; the grass in it had just taken a start, and was beautifully fresh; and very thickly growing amongst the grass was the purple flowered *Colchicum* in full bloom. . . . The flower, if standing by itself, would be no great beauty; but contrasted with the fresh grass, which was a little shorter than itself, it was very beautiful. *William Cobbett, 1826 (Herefordshire)*

A lovely day. Read Boswell in the house in the morning, and after dinner under the bright yellow leaves of the orchard. The pear trees a bright yellow. The apple trees still green. A sweet lovely afternoon.

Dorothy Wordsworth, 1800 (Westmorland)

Sharp showers; long mountains of big happed-up snow-white thundercloud, glossed with silvery shadows, and a gay dazzling invisible blue light playing on them.

Gerard Manley Hopkins, 1873 (Surrey)

I got up at 6 o'clock as the sun was rising behind the Tors [at Lynton]. The house was silent and no one seemed to be about. I unlocked the door and let myself out into the garden. It was one of the loveliest mornings that ever dawned upon this world. A heavy dew had fallen in the night and as I wandered down the beautiful winding terraced walks every touch sent a shower from the great blue globes of the hydrangeas, and on every crimson fuchsia pendant flashed a diamond dew drop.

The clear pure crisp air of the early morning blew fresh and exhilarating as the breeze came sweet from the sea.

Francis Kilvert, 1873 (North Devon)

Papilio Atalanta [Red Admiral] abounds.

Gilbert White, 1772 (Hampshire)

Gathered many of the baking pears to disburthen the boughs, and keep them from breaking.

Gilbert White, 1788 (Hampshire)

Observed the great half moon setting behind the mountain ridge, and watched the shapes its various segments presented as it slowly sunk—first, the foot of a boot, all but the heel—then, a little pyramid—then a star of the first magnitude, indeed it was not distinguishable from the Evening Star at its largest—then rapidly a smaller, a small, a very small star—and as it diminished in size, so it grew paler in tint—and now where is it? Unseen; but a little fleecy cloud hangs above the mountain ridge, and is rich—with an amber light. *S. T. Coleridge, 1801 (Cumberland)*

SEPTEMBER 16

Pleasant mild autumn, many mushrooms, smoke from cottage gardens, chilly evenings, etc.
D. H. Lawrence, 1919 (Berkshire)

SEPTEMBER 17

Full moon. The creeping fogs in the pastures are very picturesque and amusing and represent arms of the sea, rivers, and lakes. *Gilbert White, 1777 (Hampshire)*

Fine.—Chestnuts as bright as coals or spots of vermilion.
Gerard Manley Hopkins, 1868 (Surrey)

SEPTEMBER 18

I sit with all the windows and the door [of the greenhouse] wide open, and am regaled with the scent of every flower in a garden as full of flowers as I have known how to make it. We keep no bees, but if I lived in a hive I should hardly hear more of their music. All the bees in the neighbourhood resort to a bed of mignonette, opposite to the window;

and pay me for the honey they get out of it by a hum,
which, though rather monotonous, is as agreeable to my
ear as the whistling of my linnets.

William Cowper, 1784 (Buckinghamshire)

What dreadful hot weather we have!—It keeps one in a
continual state of inelegance.   *Jane Austen, 1796 (Kent)*

SEPTEMBER 19

Stormy all night. Aequinoctial weather.

Gilbert White, 1770 (Hampshire)

Ivy begins to blow on Nore-hill and is frequented by wasps.
Paid for a wasps nest, full of young.

Gilbert White, 1783 (Hampshire)

A beautful rainbow on Skiddaw—the foot of the arch in
the third field under Ormathwaite, the other foot just under
the nearest part of Skiddaw Dodd—the height of the arch
just in the half way height of Skiddaw Tent—it faded away
into a green reflection preserving its figure, yet so that if I
had not seen it before, I should not have thought it a
rainbow.   *S. T. Coleridge, 1800 (Cumberland)*

The wind grumbled and made itself miserable all last night,
and this morning it is still howling as ill-naturedly as ever,
and roaring and rumbling in the chimneys. The tide is
far out, but, from an upper window, I fancied, at intervals,
that I could see the plash of the surf-wave on the distant
limit of the sand; perhaps, however, it was only a gleam on
the sky. . . . Gray, sullen clouds hang about the sky, or
sometimes cover it with a uniform dullness; at other times,
the portions towards the sun gleam almost lightsomely;
now there may be an airy glimpse of clear blue sky in a
fissure of the clouds; now, the very brightest of sunshine

comes out all of a sudden, and gladdens everything. The breadth of sands has a various aspect, according as there are pools or moisture enough to glisten, or a drier tract; and where the light gleams along a yellow ridge or bar, it is like sunshine itself. . . . By seven o'clock pedestrians began to walk along the promenade, close-buttoned against the blast; later a single bathing-machine got under way, by means of a horse, and travelled forth seaward; but within what distance it finds the invisible margin I cannot say,—at all events, it looks like a dreary journey.

Nathaniel Hawthorne, 1856 (Lancashire)

SEPTEMBER 20

Bright. Out to gather mushrooms for breakfast.

John Ruskin, 1869 (Denmark Hill, Surrey)

SEPTEMBER 21

A robin sang all his note during Divine Service in the body of the church. *Richard Hayes, 1766 (Kent)*

. . . we wound up a chalky precipice of great sweep and length, with steep downs rising over it; sheep on the summit 'showing themselves against the sky. A fine moon rose, and lighted us over the downs to Horndon. Heard only the sheep-bells, as the shepherd was folding his flocks, and they came down from the hills.

Ann Radcliffe, 1798 (Hampshire)

Our thatched roof of rusted gold . . .

William Blake, 1800 (Sussex)

Another dense white fog which cleared off to cloudless blue and brilliant sunshine at 11. . . . Went to the Bronith. People at work in the orchard gathering up the windfall apples for early cider. The smell of the apples very strong. Beyond the orchards the lone aspen was rustling loud and mournfully a lament for the departure of summer. Called on the old soldier. He was with his wife in the garden digging and gathering red potatoes which turned up very large and sound. . . . The great round red potatoes lay thick, fresh and clean on the dark newly turned mould . . . the sun grew low . . . we heard the distant shots at partridges.

Francis Kilvert, 1870 (Radnorshire)

SEPTEMBER 22

Great dew, cold air, cloudless. *Gilbert White, 1786 (Surrey)*

Sat on the deck [en route to the Isle of Wight from Portsmouth]; a fine view of the town, the hospital, the forts and harbour, as we sailed out, the sea not rough. Hear the *he-hoes* of the sailors, afar in the channel, and the boatswains's shrill whistle. Past through a part of the fleet; saw Sir Sidney Smith's fine ship, of immense size, with many other large ones round it. A cloudy sunset, but a gleam came out that fell upon the distant town and harbour, lighted up the sea, and touched the dark polished sides of all the ships.   *Ann Radcliffe, 1798 (The Solent)*

SEPTEMBER 23

Begin to light fires in the parlour.

Gilbert White, 1781 (Hampshire)

Black snails lie out, and copulate. Vast swagging clouds.

Gilbert White, 1783 (Hampshire)

[Returning from the Isle of Wight to Portsmouth] . . . a broad moon rising over the ships at Spithead. Passed through the fleet. Heard voices talking far off over the dim waves, and sometimes laughter and joviality; especially as we passed near a large ship where lights in the great cabin high above told of the Captain and cheer. Distant lights appearing from the ships successively, as the evening deepened, like glow-worms, and dotting the water far around. As we drew near the shore, the music of French horns sounded with faint and melancholy sweetness; discovered at last to come from Monckton Fort. Landed after an hour and a half, at the rampart steps.

Ann Radcliffe, 1798 (The Solent)

The villagers of Felpham are not meer Rustics; they are polite and modest. Meat is cheaper than in London, but the sweet air and the voices of winds, trees and birds, and the odours of the happy ground, makes it a dwelling for immortals. Work will go on here with God speed.—A roller and two harrows lie before my window. I met a plow on my first going out at my gate the first morning after my arrival, and the Plowboy said to the Plowman, 'Father, The Gate is Open.'   *William Blake, 1800 (Sussex)*

SEPTEMBER 24

First saw the Northern Lights. My eye was caught by beams of light and dark very like the crown of horny rays the sun makes behind a cloud. At first I thought of silvery cloud until I saw that these were more luminous and did not dim the clearness of the stars in the Bear. They rose slightly radiating thrown out from the earthline. Then I saw soft pulses of light one after another rise and pass upwards arched in shape but waveringly and with the arch broken. They seemed to float, not following the warp of the

sphere as falling stars look to do but free though con-
centrical with it. This busy working of nature wholly
independent of the earth and seeming to go on in a strain
of time not reckoned by our reckoning of days and years
but simpler and as if correcting the preoccupation of the
world by being preoccupied with and appealing to and
dated to the day of judgement was like a new witness to
God and filled me with delightful fear.

Gerard Manley Hopkins, 1870 (Lancashire)

Very bright and clear. All the landscape had a beautiful
liquid cast of blue. Many-coloured smokes in the valley,
grey from the Denbigh limekiln, yellow and lurid from the
two kilns perhaps on the shoulders of a hill, blue from a
bonfire.   *Gerard Manley Hopkins, 1874 (Denbighshire)*

A day of exceeding and almost unmatched beauty. . . . A
warm delicious calm and sweet peace brooded breathless
over the mellow sunny autumn afternoon and the happy
stillness was broken only by the voices of children black-
berry gathering in an adjoining meadow and the sweet
solitary singing of a robin. . . . Near the entrance to the
village of Kington St Michael I fell in with a team of red
oxen, harnessed coming home from plough with chains
rattling and the old ploughman riding the fore ox. . . .

When I returned home at night the good Vicar accompanied me as far as the Plough Inn. The moon was at the
full. The night was sweet and quiet. Overhead was the vast
fleecy sky in which the moon was riding silently and the
stillness was broken only by the occasional pattering of an
acorn or a chestnut through the leaves to the ground.

Francis Kilvert, 1874 (Wiltshire)

SEPTEMBER 25

Hedge-sparrow begins its winter note.

Gilbert White, 1771 (Hampshire)

Vast tempest in the night that broke boughs from the trees, and blowed down much of the apples and pears.

Gilbert White, 1772 (Hampshire)

SEPTEMBER 26

Took a walk in the fields, heard the harvest cricket and shrew-mouse uttering their little chickering songs among the crackling stubble.   *John Clare, 1824 (Northants)*

SEPTEMBER 27

Very early on some of these days the morning mist looked like water quite still and clouded by milk or soda.

Gerard Manley Hopkins, 1868 (Surrey)

SEPTEMBER 28

. . . to Caerwys wood, a beautiful place. The day being then dark and threatening we walked some time under a grey light more charming than sunshine falling through boughs and leaves.

Gerard Manley Hopkins, 1874 (Denbighshire)

SEPTEMBER 29

After a most tremendous storm of hail: the lower half of the lake bright silver; over it and intercepting Borrodale a *thick palpable blue* up to the moon, save that at the very top of the blue the clouds rolled lead-coloured. Small detachments of these clouds running in thick flakes near the moon, and drinking its light in amber and white.— The Moon in a clear azure sky—the Mountains seen indeed, and only seen—I never saw aught so sublime!

S. T. Coleridge, 1800 (Cumberland)

Took a walk in the fields, saw an old wood-stile taken away from a favourite spot which it had occupied all my life. The posts were overgrown with ivy and it seem'd so akin to nature and the spot where it stood as tho' it had taken on a lease for an undisturb'd existence. It hurt me to see it was gone.   *John Clare, 1824 (Northants)*

A second pool [below a waterfall on the Caldew] still more beautiful and wide and green and deep, and as sweetly o'er-canopied by limes and ashes, the limes absolutely *showering* their yellow leaves.

S. T. Coleridge, 1803 (Cumberland)

SEPTEMBER 30

Lovely weather, red even. True Michaelmas summer.

Gilbert White, 1783 (Hampshire)

It rained very hard. Rydale was extremely wild. . . . We sate quietly and comfortably by the fire.

Dorothy Wordsworth, 1800 (Westmorland)

The last day in September—*immensely* cold, a kind of solid cold outside the windows. . . . *Don't* read this. Do you hear that train whistle and now the leaves—the dry leaves —and now the fire—fluttering and creaking.

Why *doesn't* she bring the lamps?

Katherine Mansfield, 1918 (Hampstead)

OCTOBER

OCTOBER 1

A fine morning, a showery night. The lake still in the
morning; in the forenoon flashing light from the beams of
the sun, as it was ruffled by the wind.

Dorothy Wordsworth, 1800 (Grasmere, Westmorland)

OCTOBER 2

A very rainy morning. We walked after dinner to observe
the torrents . . . the lichens are now coming out afresh, I
carried home a collection in the afternoon. We had a
pleasant conversation about the manners of the rich—
avarice, inordinate desires, and the effeminacy, unnatural-
ness, and the unworthy objects of education . . . a showery
evening. The moonlight lay upon the hills like snow.

Dorothy Wordsworth, 1800 (Westmorland)

OCTOBER 3

The shining purity of the lake [Derwentwater], just ruffled
by the breeze enough to show it is alive, reflecting rocks,
wood, fields and inverted tops of mountains. . . . In the evening walk'd alone down to the Lake . . . after sunset and saw
the solemn colouring of the night draw on, the last gleam
of sunshine fading away on the hill-tops, the deep serene of
the waters, and the long shadows of the mountains thrown
across them, till they nearly touched the hithermost shore.
At distance heard the murmur of many waterfalls not

audible in the day-time. Wished for the Moon, but she was *dark to me and silent, hid in her vacant inter-lunar cave.*

Thomas Gray, 1769 (Westmorland)

The cat frolicks, and plays with the fallen leaves. Acorns innumerable. *Gilbert White, 1783 (Hampshire)*

OCTOBER 4

Mushrooms abound. Made catchup.

Gilbert White, 1779 (Hampshire)

A mournful splendour in the brilliant gold of the sloes and the crimson leaves of the pear trees.

Francis Kilvert, 1871 (Radnorshire)

OCTOBER 5

A goldencrested wren had got into my room at night and circled round dazzled by the gaslight on the white cieling; when caught even and put out it would come in again. Ruffling the crest which is mounted over the crown and eyes like beetlebrows, I smoothed and fingered the little orange and yellow feathers which are hidden in it. Next morning I found many of these about the room and enclosed them in a letter to Cyril [his brother] on his wedding day. *Gerard Manley Hopkins, 1872 (Lancashire)*

OCTOBER 6

. . . arrived at Grasmere at about 6 o'clock on Wednesday evening. . . . I cannot describe what I felt. . . . We went by candle light into the garden, and were astonished at the growth of the brooms, Portugal laurels, etc. etc. etc.

Dorothy Wordsworth, 1802 (Westmorland)

OCTOBER 7

The sun had never once been overshadowed by a cloud
during the whole of our progress from the centre of Borrodale; at the summit of the Pike[1] there was not a breath of
air to stir even the papers which we spread out containing
our food. There we ate our dinner in summer warmth; and
the stillness seemed to be not of this world. We paused and
kept silence to listen, and not a sound of any kind was to
be heard. We were far above the reach of the cataracts of
Scaw Fell; and not an insect was there to hum in the air.
                    Dorothy Wordsworth, 1818 (Cumberland)

For some time I have been trying to find the right word
for the shimmering glancing twinkling movement of the
poplar leaves in the sun and wind. This afternoon I saw the
word written on the poplar leaves. It was 'dazzle'. The
dazzle of the poplars.   *Francis Kilvert, 1874 (Radnorshire)*

OCTOBER 8

Earthed up the celeri, which is very gross, and large.
                    Gilbert White, 1791 (Hampshire)

A very mild moonlight night. Glow-worms everywhere.
                    Dorothy Wordsworth, 1800 (Westmorland)

OCTOBER 9

There was a frost in the night and this morning the tops
of the poplar spires are touched, are turned to finest gold.
                    Francis Kilvert, 1871 (Radnorshire)

[1] Scafell Pike, highest point in England (3,210 feet).

Full moon. Sweet moonshine.

Gilbert White, 1783 (Hampshire)

The first snow fell on Skiddaw.

S. T. Coleridge, 1800 (Cumberland)

A fine October morning. . . . After dinner we walked up Greenhead Gill in search of a sheepfold. . . . The colours of the mountains soft and rich, with orange fern; the cattle pasturing upon the hill-tops; kites sailing in the sky above our heads; sheep bleating and in lines and chains and patterns scattered over the mountains. They come down and feed on the little green islands in the beds of torrents, and so may be swept away. The sheepfold is falling away. It is built nearly in the form of a heart unequally divided. Look down the brook, and see the drops rise upwards and sparkle in the air at the little falls. . . .

Dorothy Wordsworth, 1800 (Westmorland)

A beautiful day. We walked to the Easedale hills to hunt waterfalls. William and Mary left me sitting on a stone in the solitary mountains, and went to Easedale tarn. I grew chilly and followed them.

Dorothy Wordsworth, 1802 (Westmorland)

Ingleborough . . . was completely wrapped in clouds, all but its summit; which might have been easily mistaken for a long black cloud too, fraught with an approaching storm.

Thomas Gray, 1769 (West Riding)

We pulled apples after dinner, a large basket full. We walked before tea by Bainriggs to observe the many-coloured foliage. The oaks dark green with some yellow leaves, the birches generally still green, some near the water yellowish, the sycamore crimson and crimson-tufted, the mountain ash a deep orange, the common ash lemon colour, but many ashes still fresh in their summer green.

Dorothy Wordsworth, 1800 (Westmorland)

OCTOBER 13

Stormy winds, and gluts of rain.

Gilbert White, 1771 (Hampshire)

We saw several redwings among the bushes on the north side of the common. There were swallows about the village at the same time: so that summer and winter birds of passage were seen on the same day.

Gilbert White, 1787 (Hampshire)

OCTOBER 14

Smooth, white, satin-like trunks of holly, and noble birch, a foot or more in diameter, exquisite in variable sunlight. Rainbow staying long on northern shore. Helvellyn lovely beyond. *John Ruskin, 1873 (Coniston Lake, Lancashire)*

Rooks and jackdaws in grass, large flock all squatting facing gale and calmly feeding. . . . Put out hand for the sunshine to fall on it. Dipping in sea, crumbling earth, touching thyme. *Richard Jefferies, 1881 (Sussex?)*

OCTOBER 15

The beeches on the hanger, and the maples in my fields are
now beautifully tinged, and afford a lovely picturesque
scape, very engaging to the imagination.

Gilbert White, 1775 (Hampshire)

Hunter's moon. Much lightening and distant thunder.

Gilbert White, 1780 (Hampshire)

OCTOBER 16

Worked on my picture; painted nasturtiums; saw a stoat
run into a hole in the garden wall; went up to it and
endeavoured to lure the little beast out by mimicking a
rat's or mouse's squeak. . . . Succeeded, to my astonishment.
He came half out of the hole and looked in my face, within
easy reach.   *John Everett Millais, 1851 (Surrey)*

Sitting for an hour on the bank in the lane under Knight's
Hill, the ground covered with gossamer, all the fields
rippling with a stream of sunshine like a lake, yet no per-
ceptible wind.   *John Ruskin, 1858 (Denmark Hill, Surrey)*

OCTOBER 17

Two woodpeckers, green as parroquets. The setting sun, the
fiery ferns, the golden-russet beechen-leaves.

William Allingham, 1863 (New Forest, Hampshire)

OCTOBER 18

St. Luke's Day. This week has indeed been the summer of
St. Luke. Five of us drove in the waggonette to Oxwich
Bay. . . . We had a merry windy luncheon on the bank near

the churchyard gate, and great fun and famous laughing. An E. wind was blowing fresh and strong, the sea was rolling in grey and yeasty, and in a splendid sunburst the white seagulls were running and feeding on the yellow sands. A wild merry happy day.

Francis Kilvert, 1878 (Gower Peninsula, Glamorgan)

OCTOBER 19

Slanting pillars of light, like ladders up to heaven, their base always a field of vivid green sunshine. . . . A grey day, windy—the vale, like a place in Faery, with the autumnal colours, the orange, the red-brown, the crimson, the light yellow, the yet lingering green, beeches and birches, as they were blossoming fire and gold!—And the sun in slanting pillars, or illuminated small parcels of mist, or single spots of softest greyish light, now racing, now slowly gliding, now stationary—the mountains cloudy—the lake has been a mirror so very clear, that the water became almost invisible—and now it rolls in white breakers, like a sea; and the wind snatches up the water, and drifts it like snow—and now the rain storm pelts against my study window.

S. T. Coleridge, 1803 (Derwentwater, Cumberland)

I want to get to my easel in Town—and not to witness the rotting melancholy dissolution of the trees etc—which two months ago were so beautiful.

John Constable, 1823 (Hampstead)

Cobalt blue was poured on the hills bounding the valley of the Clwyd and far in the south spread a bluish damp, but all the nearer valley was showered with tapered diamond flakes of fields in purple and brown and green.

Gerard Manley Hopkins, 1874 (Denbighshire)

OCTOBER 20

My 30th. birthday[1]—a windy, showery day—with great columns of misty sunshine travelling along the lake toward Borrodale, the heavens a confusion of white clouds in masses, and bright blue sky. . . . The birches, auburn and gold, shew themselves among the oak grove—the white flossy sun-mist floats along, and now Borrodale looks thro' it. The upper segment of the arch of the sky is all blue, bright blue—and the descent on all sides white massy clouds, thrusting their heads into the blue, in mountain shapes. *S. T. Coleridge, 1802 (Derwentwater, Cumberland)*

OCTOBER 21

A drisling rain. Heavy masses of shapeless vapour upon the mountains . . . the birds are singing in the tender rain, as if it were the rain of April, and the decaying foliage were the flowers and blossoms. The pillar of smoke from the chimney rises up in the mist, and is just distinguishable from it. . . . (Cleared up. The last thin fleeces on the bathed fells.) *S. T. Coleridge, 1803 (Cumberland)*

A Spanish chestnut and two elms in the ground seem to fill the air up with an equable clear ochre.
Gerard Manley Hopkins, 1868 (Surrey)

OCTOBER 22

Thursday evening, $\frac{1}{2}$ past 6. All the mountains black and tremendously obscure, except Swinside. . . . At this time I saw one after the other, nearly in the same place, two perfect Moon Rainbows. . . . It was grey-moonlight-mist-color. *S. T. Coleridge, 1801 (Cumberland)*

---

[1] Coleridge's birthday was really 21 October. For some reason he was always convinced it was a day earlier.

OCTOBER 23

Fallows in a sad, wet, weedy condition: scarce any wheat
sown.   *Gilbert White, 1768 (Hampshire)*

OCTOBER 24

Does not the cathedral [Salisbury] look beautiful among
the golden foliage? Its solitary grey must sparkle in it.
                                        John Constable, 1821

OCTOBER 25

Hard frost, thick ice. In my way to Newton I was covered
with snow! Snow covers the ground, and trees!!
                              Gilbert White, 1784 (Hampshire)

Aspens—one a lovely light yellow—the other red, or rather
poppy-color'd.   *S. T. Coleridge, 1799 (North Riding)*

A damp warm morning steaming with heat, the outer air
like a hothouse, the inner air colder, and in consequence
the old thick panelled walls of the front rooms streaming
with the warm air condensed on the cold walls. . . . The
afternoon was so gloomy that I was obliged for the first
time to have lights in the pulpit.
                              Francis Kilvert, 1874 (Wiltshire)

OCTOBER 26

If a masterly landscape painter was to take our hanging
woods in their autumnal colours, persons unacquainted
with the country would object to the strength and deepness

of the tints, and would pronounce, at an exhibition, that they were heightened and shaded beyond nature.

Gilbert White, 1783 (Hampshire)

A yellow shower of leaves is falling continually from all the trees in the country. . . . The consideration of my short continuance here, which was once grateful to me, now fills me with regret. I would live and live always.

William Cowper, 1790 (Buckinghamshire)

OCTOBER 27

An enormous quantity of withered leaves, too damp to rustle, strewing the paths. . . . The pastures look just as green as ever,—a deep, bright verdure, that seems almost sunshine in itself, however sombre the sky may be.

Nathaniel Hawthorne, 1857 (Warwickshire)

OCTOBER 28

River Greta near its fall into the Tees. . . . Black round spots from 5 to 18 in the decaying leaf of the sycamore.

S. T. Coleridge, 1799 (North Riding)

Walk alone into Forest . . . spindle tree seeds; maple yellow like a ripe quince.

William Allingham, 1868 (New Forest, Hampshire)

OCTOBER 29

Wonderful downpour of leaf: when the morning sun began to melt the frost they fell at one touch and in a few minutes a whole tree was flung of them; they lay masking and papering the ground at the foot. Then the tree seems to be looking down on its cast self as blue sky on snow after a long fall, its losing, its doing.

Gerard Manley Hopkins, 1873 (Surrey)

OCTOBER 30

Larches turn yellow; ash leaves fall; the hanger gets thin.
Gilbert White, 1788 (Hampshire)

It is a breathless, grey day, that leaves the golden woods of autumn quiet in their own tranquillity, stately and beautiful in their decaying; the lake is a perfect mirror.
Dorothy Wordsworth, 1802 (Grasmere, Westmorland)

Glowing soft red clouds on blue.
John Ruskin, 1870 (Denmark Hill, Surrey)

OCTOBER 31

Took a walk, got some branches of the spindle tree with its pink-color'd berries that shine beautifully in the pale sun.
John Clare, 1824 (Northants)

A very fine moonlight night—The moon shone like herrings in the water.
Dorothy Wordsworth, 1800 (Grasmere, Westmorland)

The full moon glided on behind a black cloud. And what then? And who cared?
S. T. Coleridge, 1803 (Cumberland)

NOVEMBER

NOVEMBER 1

Wind chill as a snow wind, yet fresh; light glary roads, damp and with a spotted *plage* of decaying leaves in the mud; the pebbles washed clean on the watershed of the roads, the sand washed from them lying in the valleys by the kerbstone.   *James Smetham, 1873 (Middlesex)*

The N. Aurora made a particular appearance, forming itself into a broad, red fiery belt, which extended from E. to W. across the welkin; but the moon rising at about 10 o'the clock, in unclouded majesty, on the E. put an end to this grand, but aweful, meteorous phenomenon.
Gilbert White, 1787 (Hampshire)

NOVEMBER 2

Leaves fall very fast. My hedges shew beautiful lights, and shades: the yellow of the tall maples makes a fine contrast against the green hazels.   *Gilbert White, 1780 (Hampshire)*

Grey, blackish, damp, wretched morning; miserable foggy day.   *John Ruskin, 1857 (Denmark Hill, Surrey)*

NOVEMBER 3

Sea-gulls, winter-mews, haunt the fallows.
Gilbert White, 1777 (Hampshire)

. . . the strange hoarse belling of the buck, the fluttering of the coot as she skimmed the water with her melancholy note, the cry of the swans across the lake, the clicking of the reels as the fishermen wound up or let out their lines, the soft murmur of the woods, the quiet rustle of the red and golden drifts of beech leaves, the rush of the waterfall, the light tread of the dappled herd of deer dark and dim glancing across the green glades from shadow into sunlight and rustling under the beeches, and the merry voices of the Marquis's children at play.

Francis Kilvert, 1874 (Wiltshire)

The horse-chestnut buds at end of boughs; tree quite bare of leaves; all sticky, colour of deep varnish. . . . Still day: the earth holds its breath.   *Richard Jefferies, 1878 (Surrey)*

NOVEMBER 4

The wintry and huge constellation, Orion, begins now to make his appearance in the evening, exhibiting his enormous figure in the E.

Gilbert White, 1781 (Hampshire)

William went to the Tarn, afterwards to the top of Seat Sandal. He was obliged to lie down in the tremendous wind. The snow blew from Helvellyn horizontally like smoke—the spray of the unseen waterfall like smoke.

Dorothy Wordsworth, 1800 (Westmorland)

It is raining in torrents. The light is greenish and unnatural, objects being seen as through water. A roar of rain in the plantation, and a rush near at hand, yet not a breath of wind. A silver finger hangs from the eaves of the house to the ground. A flash and then thunder.

Thomas Hardy, 1873 (Dorset)

NOVEMBER 5

A grand crossing in bright green waves and golden light; a sunset like England and Venice in one. Lasting at least half an hour in full scarlet, only passing from fiery scarlet to ruby scarlet, dark on the green sky, and so into crimson; the whole in majestic depth of tone though so pure, so that the first gas lamps were bright against it while still ruby.   *John Ruskin, 1880 (Dover–Calais)*

NOVEMBER 6

There was a most violent gale of wind this morning early about 3 o'clock, continued more than an hour. It waked me. It also shook the house. It greatly frighted our maids in the garrett. Some limbs of trees blown down in my garden. Many windmills blown down.

James Woodforde, 1795 (Norfolk)

The oaks are beginning to turn reddish brown and the winds have stripped some nearly bare. The underwood's last leaves are in their gayest yellows. Thus autumn seems to put on bridal colours for a shroud.

John Clare, 1824 (Northants)

A lovely afternoon of the Martinmas summer. . . . On all sides the green meadows were illuminated by the golden light of the yellow elms and the red beeches. . . . The old grey manor house and church tower stood framed as in a picture by the golden elms. It was a beautiful pastoral scene, calm and peaceful. Suddenly someone began playing a beautiful air upon a horn in front of Langley House.

Francis Kilvert, 1874 (Wiltshire)

Mary drove me all in the rain to Basingstoke, and still more all in the rain back again, because it rained harder.

Jane Austen, 1796 (Hampshire)

A cold rainy morning. William still unwell. I working and reading *Amelia*. The Michaelmas daisy droops, the pansies are full of flowers, the ashes opposite are green all but one, but they have lost many of their leaves. The copses are quite brown. *Dorothy Wordsworth, 1800 (Westmorland)*

NOVEMBER 8

A rainy morning. A whirlwind came that tossed about the leaves, and tore off the still green leaves of the ashes. . . . The whole face of the country in a winter covering. We went early to bed.

Dorothy Wordsworth, 1800 (Westmorland)

Brilliant sun, black cloud and slight shower. The column of a rainbow arch sprung up out of Herefordshire from among the blue hills and golden oaks tipped with sunlight.

Francis Kilvert, 1871 (Radnorshire)

NOVEMBER 9

Lime-trees' leaves fall all at once. Floods: torrents and cataracts in the lanes. *Gilbert White, 1770 (Hampshire)*

Wednesday night, 45 minutes past 6—the town [Keswick] with lighted windows and noise of the *clogged* passengers in the streets—sound of the unseen river—mountains scarcely perceivable except by eyes long used to them, and supported by the images of memory flowing in on the impulses of immediate impression—the sky black clouds, two or three dim untwinkling stars, like full stops on damp paper—and large stains and spreads of sullen white, like a tunic of white wool seen here and there thro' a torn and tattered coat of black. *S. T. Coleridge, 1803 (Cumberland)*

When I drive across this country, with autumn falling and rustling to pieces, I am so sad, for my country, for this great wave of civilisation, 2000 years, which is now collapsing, that it is hard to live. So much beauty and pathos of old things passing away and no new things coming: this house [Garsington Manor]—it is England—my God, it breaks my soul—their England, these shafted windows, the elm-trees, the blue distance—the past, the great past, crumbling down, breaking down, not under the force of the coming birds, but under the weight of many exhausted lovely yellow leaves, that drift over the lawn, and over the pond, like the soldiers, passing away, into winter and the darkness of winter—no, I can't bear it. For the winter stretches ahead, where all vision is lost and all memory dies out. *D. H. Lawrence, 1915 (Oxfordshire)*

NOVEMBER 10

I baked bread. A fine clear frosty morning. We walked after dinner to Rydale village. Jupiter over the hilltops, the only star, like a sun, flashed out at intervals from behind a black cloud. *Dorothy Wordsworth, 1800 (Westmorland)*

Thursday night, $\frac{1}{4}$ after 7. The sky covered with stars; the wind up; right opposite my window, over Brandelhow . . . an enormous black cloud exactly in the shape of an egg—this the only cloud in all the sky—impressed me with a daemoniacal grandeur.—O for change of weather!
S. T. Coleridge, 1803 (Cumberland)

11 o'clock. Perfectly starless—almost black—only over Borrodale the clouds are pallidezza affumicata—a dingy paleness—calm as death. The Greta always sounding.

S. T. Coleridge, 1803 (Cumberland)

Bright orange dawn passing up through greenish amber into purple. Moon *glitteringly* bright; morning star large like a cross, dwindling to a point as the day rose. . . . Men mowing, birds singing, air quite mild. It gets misty with white clouds as the sun rises. Mist gathers. It turned out a fine day, the sun warm at ten o'clock on the arbutus' scarlet berries and white blossoms, and coral of the holly, the fuchsias still in flower: leaves full and even green on many trees. White on line of cloud on Norwood hills.

John Ruskin, 1857 (Denmark Hill, Surrey)

Fine; elm leaves very crisp and chalky and yellow, a scarlet brightness against the blue. Sparks of falling leaves streaming down and never stopping from far off.

Gerard Manley Hopkins, 1873 (Surrey)

On the hills snow lying and the mountains covered from head to foot. . . . I went with Mr. Hughes up Moel y Parch, from the top of which we had a noble view, but the wind was very sharp. Snowdon and all the range reminded me of the Alps: they looked like a stack of rugged white flint, specked and streaked with black, in many places chiselled and channelled.

Gerard Manley Hopkins, 1874 (Denbighshire)

A flooded river after the incessant rains of yesterday. Lumps of froth float down like swans in front of our house.

At the arches of the large stone bridge the froth has accumulated and lies like hillocks of salt against the bridge; then the arch chokes, and after a silence coughs out the air and froth, and gurgles on.

Thomas Hardy, 1877 (Dorset)

NOVEMBER 13

Nuthatches rap about on the trees. Crocuses begin to sprout. The leaves of the medlar-tree are now turned of a bright yellow.   *Gilbert White, 1776 (Hampshire)*

The runs dusty, and the chaises run on the summer tracks, on the downs. Lovely clouds, and sky.

Gilbert White, 1783 (Hampshire)

Out after midnight to look for meteors, see many streaming like fiery arrows, mostly from east to west.

William Allingham, 1866 (Hampshire)

The first frost of autumn. Outdoor folk look reflective. The scarlet runners are dishevelled: geraniums wounded in the leaf, open-air cucumber leaves have collapsed like green umbrellas with all the stays broken.

Thomas Hardy, 1872 (Dorset)

NOVEMBER 14

Hedges, ferns, yellow oakleaves, harebells, children sweeping up fallen leaves. *William Allingham, 1867 (Hampshire)*

NOVEMBER 15

The hills thro' the fog appeared like vast mountains.

Gilbert White, 1785 (Hampshire)

Paths greazy from the frost. Raked, and swept up the leaves in my outlet. The hanger naked.

Gilbert White, 1790 (Hampshire)

Winter is established.   *Gilbert White, 1783 (Hampshire)*

What fine weather this is! Not very becoming perhaps early in the morning, but very pleasant out of doors at noon, and very wholesome—at least everybody fancies so, and imagination is everything.

Jane Austen, 1798 (Hampshire)

The fog has now closed over the Lake [Ullswater], and we wander in darkness, save that the mist is here and there prettily coloured by the wither'd fern, over which it hovers.

S. T. Coleridge, 1799 (Westmorland)

Cottages [at Laugharne] favourable only to vegetable life— Hot-bed of wild weeds on their roofs and ivy on their walls—but the shrivelled shrimps of cold and hunger— swarthied tenants.

> Here
> lieth the Body
> of Marg. Bevan, who
> departed this Life the 9th. day of
> June 1727, Aged 19 years

Here lie 2 Sisters side by side
They sleep and take their rest,
Till Christ shall raise them up again
To live among the Blest—

At the foot of a grave a lower stone, nearly the same shape, only with

Here
lyeth the Body of Elizabeth
Bevan, who died the 3rd.
of June, 1725, aged 22 years.

At the last day I am sure
I shall appear to meet with
Jesus Christ, my saviour dear
Where I do hope to live with him
in bliss. O what a Joy at my
last hour was this!

While I took the copy, the groundsel showered its white beard on me. Groundsel and fern on the grave, and the thorns growing that had been bound over it—

On a square tomb as high as half up my thigh, where the tom-tits with their black velvet caps showered down the lovely yew berries on me: Here lyeth the Body of Sara and Hannah Jones the Daughters of Evan Jones and Jane his Wife. Sara Jones died January the 19th., aged 2 years and 3 months. Hannah Jones departed this Life the 8th. day of September, 1746, aged 15 years. . . .

S. T. Coleridge, 1802 (Carmarthenshire)

NOVEMBER 18

Nasturtiums blow yet; some few leaves are decayed. Grapes delicate; but many bunches decay. Paths dry.

Gilbert White, 1772 (Hampshire)

Mary and I walked as far as Sara's Gate before supper. We stood there a long time, the whole scene impressive, the mountains indistinct, the Lake [Grasmere] calm and partly ruffled. Large Island, a sweet sound of water falling into the quiet lake. A storm was gathering in Easedale, so we returned; but the moon came out, and opened to us the church and village. Helm Crag in shade, the larger mountains dappled like a sky. We stayed long upon the bridge.

Dorothy Wordsworth, 1801 (Westmorland)

NOVEMBER 19

This afternoon the weather turning suddenly very warm produced an unusual appearance; for the dew on the windows was on the *outside* of the glass, the air being warmer *abroad* than *within*.

Gilbert White, 1776 (Hampshire)

Fearfully cold. Landscape trees upon my window-panes. After breakfast chopped wood, and after that painted ivy. . . . See symptoms of a speedy finish to my background. After lunch pelted down some remaining apples in the orchard. Read Tennyson and the Thirty-Nine Articles.

John Everett Millais, 1851 (Surrey)

NOVEMBER 20

Wild wind and coursing cloud; feeble gleams of pale sky.

John Ruskin, 1875 (Oxford)

NOVEMBER 21

I noticed in the poplar above me two sorts of sound; the leaves pattering and rustling against one another, each with its separate chatter; and then as accompaniment and continuous ground-tone, the wind itself breathing audibly and caressingly between leave and round twigs and limbs.

George Sturt, 1890 (Surrey)

NOVEMBER 22

The smoke of the new lighted limekilns this evening crept along the ground in long trails: a token of a dry, heavy atmosphere.   *Gilbert White, 1788 (Hampshire)*

Very beautiful, delicately vermilion morning. Clouds moving softly from S.W. Grey day, mild. Sunny afternoon full on the golden trees; sweet twilight with new moon. (Garden spoiled by vile chrysanthemums).
          John Ruskin, 1857 (Denmark Hill, Surrey)

NOVEMBER 23

The downy seeds of Travellers Joy fill the air, and driving before a gale appear like insects on the wing. Mrs Clement brought to bed of a boy. My nephews and nieces now 53.
          Gilbert White, 1788 (Hampshire)

I went to the window to empty my urine-pot, and wondered at the simple grandeur of the view. 1. Darkness and only not utter black undistinguishableness—2. The grey-blue steely glimmer of the Greta, and the Lake [Derwentwater] —3. The black, yet form preserving mountains—4. The sky, moon-whitened there, cloud-blackened here—and yet with all its gloominess and sullenness forming a contrast with the simplicity of the landscape beneath.
          S. T. Coleridge, 1803 (Cumberland)

NOVEMBER 24

Cascades fall from the fields into the hollow lanes.
          Gilbert White, 1781 (Hampshire)

I read a little of Chaucer, prepared the goose for dinner, and then we all walked out. I was obliged to return for my fur tippet and spencer, it was so cold. . . . It was very windy, and we heard the wind everywhere about us as we went along the lane, but the walls sheltered us. . . . As we were going along we were stopped at once, at the distance perhaps of 50 yards from our favourite birch tree. It was yielding to the gusty wind with all its tender twigs, the sun shone upon it, and it glanced in the wind like a flying sunshiny shower. It was a tree in shape, with stem and branches, but it was like a Spirit of water. The sun went in, and it resumed its purplish appearance, the twigs still yielding to the wind, but not so visibly to us. The other birch trees that were near it looked bright and chearful, but it was a creature by its own self among them. . . . Catkins are coming out; palm trees budding; the alder, with its plumb-coloured buds. We came home over the stepping-stones. The Lake [Grasmere] was foamy with white waves.

Dorothy Wordsworth, 1801 (Westmorland)

Very wet. But quiet, and birds singing all sorts of delicate airs, richly, as if it were spring.

John Ruskin, 1857 (Denmark Hill, Surrey)

NOVEMBER 25

Fog, with frost. As the fog cleared away, the warm sun occasioned a prodigious reek, or steam to arise from the thatched roofs.   *Gilbert White, 1781 (Hampshire)*

NOVEMBER 26

Very dark season: dark within doors a little after 3 o'clock in the afternoon.   *Gilbert White, 1775 (Hampshire)*

Monthly roses now in bloom.

Gilbert White, 1787 (Hampshire)

NOVEMBER 27

Fierce frost. Rime hangs all day on the hanger. The hares, press'd by hunger, haunt the gardens and devour the pinks, cabbages, parsley, etc. Cats catch the red-breasts. Timothy the tortoise sleeps in the fruit-border under the wall, covered with a hen-coop, in which is a good armfull of straw. Here he will lie warm, secure, and dry. His back is partly covered with mould.

Gilbert White, 1782 (Hampshire)

Starlings in vast flights drove along like smoke . . . glimmering and shivering, dim and shadowy, now thickening, deepening, blackening.

S. T. Coleridge, 1799 (in a coach, between Westmorland and London)

NOVEMBER 28

Sunday. A perfectly divine vermilion sunrise, with crescent moon rising, called me up before coffee. Deeply thankful that blue and vermilion are still there, and my eyes still good, even to not feeling any defect in my joy in these things.   *John Ruskin, 1880 (Denmark Hill, Surrey)*

NOVEMBER 29

Snow was halfshoe deep on the hill. Distant lightening.

Gilbert White, 1779 (Hampshire)

All painted after breakfast—Hunt [Holman Hunt] at grass; myself, having nearly finished the wall, went on to complete stalk and lower leaves of Canterbury-bell in the corner. Young, who was with Hunt, said he heard the stag-hounds out; went to discover, and came running in in a state of frenzied excitement for us to see the hunt. Saw about fifty riders after the hounds, but missed seeing the stag, it having got some distance ahead. Moralised afterwards, thinking it a savage and uncivilised sport.

John Everett Millais, 1851 (Surrey)

NOVEMBER 30

Herne Hill. Bitterly cold and dark; the paper chilling my fingers. *John Ruskin, 1875 (Surrey)*

DECEMBER

DECEMBER 1

. . . this fine first of December, under an unclouded sky, and in a room full of sunshine. . . .

William Cowper, 1789 (Buckinghamshire)

Towards dark, a colourless fog, snow almost gone, and ground soft-oozy underfoot, as though the earth's skin slipped as you trod. A very dark night: no wind; church bells dinning, and myself chilly and afraid of the misty evening. *George Sturt, 1890 (Surrey)*

DECEMBER 2

Thunder and hail. Incredible quantities of rain have fallen this week. *Gilbert White, 1768 (Hampshire)*

DECEMBER 3

Down at 7 exactly, and foggy, only not cloudy. Note, there is much light in the sky even now, though not three weeks to the shortest day.

John Ruskin, 1869 (Denmark Hill, Surrey)

DECEMBER 4

Most owls seem to hoot exactly in B flat according to several pitch-pipes used in tuning of harpsichords, and as strictly at concert pitch.

Gilbert White, 1770 (Hampshire)

A gusty wind makes the raindrops hit the window in stars, and the sunshine flaps open and shut like a fan, flinging into the room a tin-coloured light.

Thomas Hardy, 1884 (Dorset)

Ice lay hidden in the green of the Brussels sprouts that we gathered for dinner.   *George Sturt, 1892 (Surrey)*

DECEMBER 5

Fetched some mulleins, foxgloves, and dwarf-laurels [spurge laurel] from the high wood and hanger; and planted them in the garden.

Gilbert White, 1783 (Hampshire)

Helen and I to Blackdown . . . she sat courageously for two hours sketching in the cold. . . . An immense level of thin cloud stretched moveless from north to south over the great Sussex landscape—green fields, houses, villages, stood forth in the sunlight; clear, remote, all silent; near at hand a bold sweeping slope of rusty fern, gorse clumps coming into Christmas blossom, mixed with a few hollies and stunted firs.   *William Allingham, 1884 (Sussex)*

DECEMBER 6

N.B. Something metallic, silver playfully and imperfectly gilt, and highly polished; or rather something mother-of-pearlish, in the sun gleams upon ice, thin ice.

S. T. Coleridge, 1803 (Cumberland)

I never saw a more straight-forward day of rain out of Cumberland, Wales, or Naples, and so dark withal I could scarcely see to read at midday, and got dreadfully low. I am ashamed to find myself so much at the mercy of a dark sky.   *John Ruskin, 1841 (Denmark Hill, Surrey)*

DECEMBER 7

Winter. The landscape has turned from a painting to an engraving: the birds that love worms fall back upon berries: the back parts of homesteads assume, in the general nakedness of the trees, a humiliating squalidness as to their details that has not been contemplated by their occupiers.

Thomas Hardy, 1886 (Dorset)

DECEMBER 8

This would have been a bright sunny day but for the interference of the fog; and before I had been out long, I actually saw the sun looking red and rayless, much like the millionth magnification of a new half-penny.

Nathaniel Hawthorne, 1857 (London)

. . . at about half past four began the Great Storm of 1872. Suddenly the wind rose up and began to roar at the Tower window and shake the panes and lash the glass with torrents of rain. It grew very dark and we struggled home in torrents of rain and tempests of wind so fearful that we could hardly force our way across the Common to the Rectory. All the evening the roaring S.W. wind raged more and more furious. It seemed as if the windows on the west side of the house must be blown in. The glass cracked and strained and bent. . . . I went out to see where the cows were, fearing that the large elms in the Avenue might fall and crush them. The trees were writhing, swaying, rocking, lashing their arms wildly and straining terribly in the tempest but I could not see that any were gone yet. The twin firs in the orchard seemed the worst off, they gave the wind such a power and purchase, with their heavy green boughs, and their tops were swaying fearfully and bending nearly double under the tremendous strain. . . . Now and then the moon looked out for a moment wild and terrified through a savage rent in the storm.

The cows were safe in the cowyard and the door shut, though how I cannot tell. They must have gone there for shelter and it seemed as if the Lord had shut them in. . . . Everything was drowned in the roar and thunder of the storm. The wind howled down the chimney, the room was full of smoke and every now and then the fire flaught out into the room in tongues of flame beaten down with a smother of sparks and smoke.

Francis Kilvert, 1872 (Wiltshire)

DECEMBER 9

Honeysuckle out and catkins hanging in the thickets.

Gerard Manley Hopkins, 1868 (Surrey)

DECEMBER 10

The blue mountains were silver ribbed with snow and looked like a dead giant lying in state—a Titan . . . home by the upper road crazy with face ache, weak and wretched, and the road never seemed to be so long. As I passed Whitty's Mill in the dusk the mill seemed to be at work. After dinner and four glasses of port I felt better.

Francis Kilvert, 1871 (Radnorshire)

DECEMBER 11

Summer-like: the air is full of gossamer, and insects.

Gilbert White, 1776 (Hampshire)

This has been a foggy morning and forenoon, snowing a little now and then, and disagreeably cold. . . . At about twelve there is a faint glow of sunlight, like the gleaming reflection from a not highly polished copper kettle.

Nathaniel Hawthorne, 1855 (Lancashire)

DECEMBER 12

A fine frosty morning—Snow upon the ground. I made bread and pies. . . . All the mountains looked like solid stone. . . . The snow hid all the grass, and all signs of vegetation, and the rocks showed themselves boldly everywhere, and seemed more stony than rock or stone. The birches on the crags beautiful, red brown and glittering. The ashes glittering spears with their upright stems. . . . We played at cards—sate up late. The moon shone upon the water [of Grasmere] below Silver-How, and above it hung, combining with Silver-How on one side, a bowl-shaped moon, the curve downwards; the white fields, glittering roof of Thomas Ashburner's house, the dark yew tree, the white fields gay and beautiful. William lay with his curtains open that he might see it.

Dorothy Wordsworth, 1801 (Westmorland)

DECEMBER 13

Ice bears: boys slide.

Gilbert White, 1775 (Hampshire)

DECEMBER 14

Dark and mild, spitting rain, great rain. Earthworms are alert, and throw up their casts this mild weather.

Gilbert White, 1774 (Hampshire)

DECEMBER 15

The mountain was veiled in a tender gauze of green mist, and a sudden burst lit the country with a strange violet glare. *Francis Kilvert, 1871 (Radnorshire)*

DECEMBER 16

A plant of misseltoe grows on a bough of the medlar: it
abounds in my hedges on the maple. The air is full of
insects. Turkies strut and gobble. Many lambs at the
Priory.   *Gilbert White, 1780 (Hampshire)*

The walks in my fields are strewed with the berries of the
misseltoe blown from the hedges.
                                 Gilbert White, 1786 (Hampshire)

DECEMBER 17

All the pink and yellow tints shine out vividly, on these
still pure frosty mornings.   *George Sturt, 1901 (Surrey)*

DECEMBER 18

Mary and William walked round the two lakes [Grasmere
and Rydal Water]. I stayed at home to make bread, cakes
and pies. I went afterwards to meet them. . . . It was a
chearful glorious day. The birches and all trees beautiful,
hips bright red, mosses green.
                           Dorothy Wordsworth, 1801 (Westmorland)

DECEMBER 19

. . . as mild a day as I ever remember. We all set out to
walk. . . . There were flowers of various kinds—the top-
most bell of a foxglove, geraniums, daisies, a buttercup in
the water . . . small yellow flowers (I do not know their
name) in the turf, a large bunch of strawberry blossoms.
                           Dorothy Wordsworth, 1802 (Westmorland)

Long Ditton. Snow on the graves. A superfluous piece of cynicism in Nature. *Thomas Hardy, 1874 (Surrey)*

December 19th or thereabouts a very fine sunrise: the higher cloud was like seams of red candle-wax.
Gerard Manley Hopkins, 1870 (Lancashire)

DECEMBER 20

I now have strawberries in bloom as white as though in the month of May, under north wall; and a young elm in beautifully green leaf, planted over the way in Elm Grove. Was it now the month of May I should soon have ripe strawberries for a dessert. Wind full south, with a very pleasant and warmish breeze such as I have felt colder in May and June. *Richard Hayes, 1772 (Kent)*

Sunday. It snowed all day.... It was a very deep snow. The brooms were very beautiful, arched feathers with wiry stalks pointed to the end, smaller and smaller. They waved gently with the weight of the snow.
Dorothy Wordsworth, 1801 (Westmorland)

DECEMBER 21

Furze is in bloom.... Shortest day.
Gilbert White, 1781 (Hampshire)

Monday 21st, being the shortest day. Mary walked to Ambleside for letters. It was a wearisome walk, for the snow lay deep upon the roads and it was beginning to thaw. I stayed at home and clapped the small linen.
Dorothy Wordsworth, 1801 (Westmorland)

On the sycamores at Castle Steps, the bark was very beautiful; green predominating, but a wonderful mauve too, with blues, yellows etc., all heightened and brilliant with a light reflected from the snow. *George Sturt, 1890 (Surrey)*

DECEMBER 22

First ice. Icicles. Ground very white. Nasturtiums cut all down, and rotten.   *Gilbert White, 1772 (Hampshire)*

Still thaw. I washed my head. William and I went to Rydale for letters, the road was covered with dirty snow, rough and rather slippery . . . a melancholy letter from Coleridge. . . . We walked home almost without speaking. . . . William walked further. When he came home he cleared a path to the necessary, called me out to see it, but before we got there a whole housetopfull of snow had fallen from the roof upon the path and it echoed in the ground beneath like a dull beating upon it. . . . We stopped to look at the stone seat at the top of the hill. There was a white cushion upon it, round at the edge like a cushion, and the rock behind looked soft as velvet, of a vivid green, and so tempting! The snow too looked as soft as a down cushion. A young foxglove, like a star, in the centre. There were a few green lichens about it, and a few withered brackens of fern here and there upon the ground near, all else was a thick snow; no footmark to it, not the foot of a sheep.
          Dorothy Wordsworth, 1801 (Westmorland)

DECEMBER 23

Before day. A lavender curtain with a pale crimson hem covers the east and shuts out the dawn.
          Thomas Hardy, 1873 (Dorset)

$\frac{1}{2}$ past 9 morning. Since the morning of the 21st., the fog has never once broken, and now is intense yellow black, the room being in pure night effect, with three candles.

As the clock struck 10, the gardeners could not see to work.   *John Ruskin, 1871 (Denmark Hill, Surrey)*

A glorious rosy morning, after a full-star night, during which I watched first the setting of a great planet, reflected in the lake like a moon, and then of the Pleiades, behind the Old Man; I watched the planet to the very edge, looked away for an instant, forgetfully, looked back, and it was gone. But the Pleiades I watched sink and disappear, one by one, exactly in the hollow of the summit above the high tarn.   *John Ruskin, 1881 (Coniston Lake, Lancashire)*

DECEMBER 24

Rydale is covered with ice, clear as polished steel, I have procured a pair of skates and to-morrow mean to give my body to the wind.
                    William Wordsworth, 1799 (Westmorland)

Christmas Eve. William is now sitting by me, at $\frac{1}{2}$ past 10 o'clock. I have been beside him ever since tea running the heel of a stocking, repeating some of his sonnets to him, listening to his own repeating, reading some of Milton's, and the *Allegro* and *Penseroso*. It is a quiet keen frost.
                    Dorothy Wordsworth, 1802 (Westmorland)

DECEMBER 25

Vast rime, strong frost, bright, and still, fog. The hanging woods when covered with a copious rime appear most beautiful and grotesque.   *Gilbert White, 1799 (Hampshire)*

I lighted my large wax-candle being Xmas Day during tea-time this afternoon for about an hour. It was very mild, thank God, to-day for this time of the year, tho' wet and very dirty walking.   *James Woodforde, 1790 (Norfolk)*

It is to-day Christmas Day, Saturday, 25th December 1802. I am thirty-one years of age. It is a dull, frosty day.
                    Dorothy Wordsworth, 1802 (Westmorland)

Saturday. Christmas Day. Gather'd a handful of daisies in full bloom—saw a woodbine and dogrose in the woods putting out in full leaf and a primrose root full of ripe flowers.   *John Clare, 1824 (Northants)*

Black rocks, breakers ghostly white, light at sea.
                    William Allingham, 1867 (Isle of Wight)

. . . intense frost. I sat down in my bath upon a sheet of thick ice which broke in the middle into large pieces whilst sharp points and jagged edges stuck all round the sides of the tub like chevaux de frise, not particularly comforting to the naked thighs. . . . The morning was most brilliant . . . the road sparkled with millions of rainbows, the seven colours gleaming in every glittering point of hoar frost.
                        Francis Kilvert, 1870 (Radnorshire)

DECEMBER 26

Did you ever know a more absolute country gentleman? Here am I come down to what you call keeping Christmas! Indeed it is not in all the forms; I have stuck no laurel and holly in my windows, I eat no turkey and chine, I have no tenants to invite. I have not brought a single soul with me. The weather is excessively stormy, but has been so warm and so entirely free from frosts the whole winter, that not only several of my honeysuckles are come out, but I have literally a blossom upon a nectarine tree, which I believe was never seen in this climate before on the 26th of December.   *Horace Walpole, 1748 (Middlesex)*

DECEMBER 27

Weather more like April than the end of December. Hedge-sparrow sings.   *Gilbert White, 1768 (Hampshire)*

Heavy rain in the night, but a lovely sunny warm morning. As I write a dew diamond is sparkling and flashing rainbows on a rose leaf outside the dining room window, a more superb diamond than any among the Crown jewels of England.   *Francis Kilvert, 1873 (Wiltshire)*

Thick snow, dazzling. Trees broken, laurels bowed to the ground, our children shovelling in the garden. Snow man.
                    William Allingham, 1886 (Surrey)

DECEMBER 28

Frost last night and this morning and all the day intense—it froze in every part of the house, even in the kitchen. . . . Meat like blocks of wood. It froze in the kitchen even by the fire in a very few minutes. . . . Giblett soup and pigg's fry for dinner to-day etc.
                    James Woodforde, 1798 (Norfolk)

An inch of snow fell last night and as we walked to Draycot to skate the snow storm began again. As we passed Langley Burrell Church we heard the strains of the quadrille band on the ice at Draycott. . . . The Lancers was beautifully skated. When it grew dark the ice was lighted with Chinese lanterns, and the intense glare of blue, green, and crimson lights and magnesium riband made the whole place as light as day. Then people skated with torches.
                    Francis Kilvert, 1870 (Wiltshire)

Yellowish haze polluting sunshine. Intense white of fresh snow everywhere and sharp frost.
                    John Ruskin, 1874 (Coniston, Lancashire)

Snow has fallen, and everything is white. It is very cold. . . . I love to close my eyes a moment and think of the land outside, white under the mingled snow and moonlight—white trees, white fields—the heaps of stone by the road-side white—snow in the furrows. . . . If he were to come I could not even hear his footsteps.

Katherine Mansfield, 1914 (Buckinghamshire)

DECEMBER 29

A thin fog upon the hills which soon disappeared. The sun shone. . . . As we ascended the hills it grew very cold and slippery. Luckily, the wind was at our backs, and helped us on. A sharp hail-shower gathered at the head of Matter-dale, and the view upwards was very grand—the wild cottages, seen through the hurrying hail-shower. The wind drove and eddied about and about, and the hills looked very large and swelling through the storm.

Dorothy Wordsworth, 1801 (Westmorland)

DECEMBER 30

Papilio Io [peacock butterfly] appears within doors, and is very brisk. *Gilbert White, 1769 (Hampshire)*

We ate some potted beef on horseback and sweet cake. We stopped our horse close to the hedge, opposite a tuft of primroses, three flowers in full blossom and a bud. They reared themselves up among the green moss. We debated long whether we should pluck them, and at last left them to live out their day, which I was right glad of at my return the Sunday following; for there they remained un-injured either by cold or wet.

Dorothy Wordsworth, 1802 (Cumberland)

Thus far have we come through the winter, on this bleak and blasty shore of the Irish Sea, where, perhaps, the drowned body of Milton's friend Lycidas might have been washed ashore more than two centuries ago. . . . It is an excessively windy place, especially here on the Promenade; always a whistle and a howl,—always an eddying gust through the corridors and chambers,—often a patter of hail or rain or snow against the windows; and in the long evenings the sounds outside are very much as if we were on shipboard in mid-ocean, with the waves dashing against the vessel's sides.

Nathaniel Hawthorne, 1856 (Southport, Lancashire)

At five minutes to midnight the bells of Chippenham church pealed out loud and clear in the frosty air. We opened a shutter and stood around listening. It was a glorious moonlit night. *Francis Kilvert, 1871 (Wiltshire)*

ON THE WRITERS

✢≫≫ ✧❊✧ ≪≪✢

WILLIAM ALLINGHAM (1824–89). Poet, chiefly remembered for 'Up the airy mountain, down the rushy glen'. His home as a boy was Ballyshannon, Co. Donegal. As a customs officer, he served for some time at Lymington on the edge of the New Forest, within visiting distance of Tennyson's home on the Isle of Wight. Tennyson was the lion and idol of his *Diary*, from which the extracts were taken.

> *February 5. May 18, 31. June 10, 28. July 15, 22. October 17, 28. November 13, 14. December 5, 25, 27.*

JANE AUSTEN (1775–1817). Hampshire was her county; she was the seventh child of the rector of the Hampshire parish of Steventon, and lies under a stone in Winchester cathedral which does not mention that she wrote novels.

Extracts from her *Letters*, 1932.

> *January 25. September 18. November 7, 17.*

WILLIAM BLAKE (1757–1827). Born, lived, and died in London. He said that nature 'put him out', which was true, but not until he had taken much of it in. He walked the fields around a smaller London, and also visited Sussex. Samuel Palmer (see below) said of the old Blake he knew, that 'to walk with him in the Country was to perceive the soul of beauty through the forms of matter'.

> *September 21, 23.*

JOHN CLARE (1793–1864). Poet, son of a farm labourer. He grew up on the border of the Fens, at Helpston in Northamptonshire, and finished his life in the public asylum at Northampton. The three forces in his poetry and mental life were joy in nature, love, and freedom. He felt himself married to nature, and his environment.

Extracts from his *Journal*, 1824–5, which has been printed in *The Prose of John Clare*, 1951.

> *January 10, 25, 31. February 4. March 11, 14. April 10, 23, 28. September 10, 26, 29. October 31. November 6. December 25.*

WILLIAM COBBETT (1766–1835). Farmer, traveller, journalist, politician, controversialist writer on many things from politics to rural economy. He was born at Farnham (where he is buried, in the churchyard), the son of a Surrey smallholder.

The extracts are from his famous *Rural Rides*, which were first published in 1830. His ideal was good country, well farmed, with a prosperous, unexploited peasantry.

> *May 7. June 24. August 2, 7, 28. September 1, 11, 13.*

SAMUEL TAYLOR COLERIDGE (1772–1834). The Devonshire-born poet of *Kubla Khan*—of imagination—was given to exploring his world on foot, and making verbal sketches at great length in his notebooks, analysing his immediate impressions and relating them to the life of the mind.

Extracts from *Anima Poetae*, 1895, his *Notebooks*, now in the course of publication, and his *Collected Letters*.

> *January 1, 3, 4, 5, 15. February 28. April 16. June 8, 18. July 19, 25, 26. August 3, 21, 24, 27. September 1, 2, 9, 15, 19, 29. October 10, 19, 20, 21, 22, 25, 28, 31. November 9, 10, 11, 17, 23, 27. December 6.*

JOHN CONSTABLE (1776–1837). One of the few English painters able to express himself in determined independent English. Bred in Suffolk, along the Essex border, liked elders in blossom, pencil-dark elms, ash trees, valleys with winding streams, locks, flashes, barges, heavy clouds, and rainbows. Unhappy in the fashionable Lake District; at home in Suffolk, Wiltshire around Salisbury, Dorset, and Hampstead Heath.

Extracts from *John Constable's Correspondence*.

> *January 20. June 17, 22. August 16, 27. September 3. October 19, 24.*

WILLIAM COWPER (1731–1800). Poet, the son of a Hertfordshire parson. 'I was a stricken deer, that left the herd'—recurrent attacks of madness meant that he withdrew to a quiet life, first at Huntingdon, then in the willow country of the Ouse, in the northern corner of Buckinghamshire. His homes there were at Olney, and afterwards at Weston Underwood, two miles away, where one thinks of him enjoying the garden, the passage of the months, and birds announcing the spring or shaking off drops of ice 'that tinkle in the withered leaves below'.

Extracts from *Correspondence*.

> *January 30. May 29. June 13, 21, 23, 25. July 3. August 3, 12, 27. September 18. October 26. December 1.*

JOHN FISHER (1788–1832). Archdeacon of Berkshire, friend of John Constable (see above), of a character no less independent. His uncle was Constable's patron, the Bishop of Salisbury; and through him Constable came to paint in Dorset, where he held livings at Osmington and Gillingham.

Extract from *John Constable's Correspondence*.

> *April 8.*

THOMAS GRAY (1716–71). The rather epicene bachelor poet of 'The Elegy in a Country Churchyard'—Stoke Poges, in which churchyard he was buried. Friend of Horace Walpole (see below). He had a love of natural history and picturesque journeying, e.g. into the Lake District and among the limestone scars of the West Riding.

Extracts from *Correspondence of Thomas Gray*.

> *January 18. February 25. April 20. June 3. October 3, 12.*

THOMAS HARDY (1840–1928). Hoped to be remembered—and he may be—as poet rather than novelist. Born and bred in a cottage under the black Dorset heaths; lived most of his life in Dorset, noticing the irony of man's situation in a witless nature, curious, beautiful, ugly, soothing, or intimidating.

Extracts from *The Life of Thomas Hardy* and *Thomas Hardy's Notebooks*.

> *January 2, 19. February 10. March 2. May 30. June 2, 9. November 4, 12, 13. December 4, 7, 19, 23.*

NATHANIEL HAWTHORNE (1804–64). American novelist, descended from a Wiltshire ancestor who reached Salem, Mass., in 1630. For five years, from 1853, he was American Consul at Liverpool. He liked to think of the body of Milton's Lycidas floating in across Southport sands, but otherwise he loathed the Mersey, the coast, the sour flatness, and the wind, slipping away, when he could, to fill his notebooks with impressions of a more genial England.

Extracts from *English Notebooks*, 1883 (but see the extended edition of 1944).

> *February 27. April 12. May 10, 27. July 4, 6. September 1, 19. October 27. December 8, 11, 31.*

RICHARD HAYES (1725–90). A considerable yeoman of Cobham in Kent, where he lived in the seventeenth-century house known as Owletts. He is buried in the Hayes vault in the churchyard.

All that survives of what must have been a remarkable diary, will be found in Ralph Arnold's *A Yeoman of Kent*, 1949.

> *January 4, 11, 21, 22, 31. February 7, 20, 23. March 9, 21. April 15, 25. May 6, 22. June 23. July 30. August 1, 2. September 13, 21.*

GERARD MANLEY HOPKINS (1844–89). Poet and Catholic priest, born at Stratford in Essex, brought up on the borders of Hampstead Heath. He made an exact passionate science of observing and analysing everything which attracted him in nature, particularly in the Midland country around Oxford, in Devonshire, in Lancashire around Stonyhurst, on the Isle of Man, and in the Vale of Clwyd (where he wrote his most ecstatic poems, within sight of the blue of the Welsh mountains).

Extracts from *The Journals and Papers of Gerard Manley Hopkins*, 1959, and *Further Letters of Gerard Manley Hopkins*, 1956.

> *January 3, 18. February 12, 23. March 2, 3, 15, 26. April 14, 15, 17, 20, 27. May 1, 3, 6, 7, 11, 17, 20, 21, 22. June 14, 16, 19, 24. July 4, 8, 9, 10, 12, 18, 23, 24, 29. August 5, 6, 7, 8, 10, 14, 18, 29. September 8, 14, 17, 24, 27, 28. October 5, 19, 21, 29. November 12. December 9, 19.*

RICHARD JEFFERIES (1848–87). Country writer, novelist, and journalist. Son of a Wiltshire farmer, grew up below the chalk downs outside Swindon, the district of his *Amateur Poacher* and *Wild Life in a Southern County*.

Extracts from *Nature Diaries*, which record experiences mainly of Surrey and Sussex.

*January 8. February 11. March 7, 31. April 6, 10, 26. May 12,
14, 18, 26. June 23, 28. July 22. August 4, 19, 23, 28, 30.
September 5. October 14.*

FRANCIS KILVERT (1840–79). Wiltshire cleric and diarist; grew
up near Chippenham, at Hardenhuish, and Langley Burrell
(where his father was rector). Curate for seven years at Clyro, in
Radnorshire, in the delectable country of the Wye, blue hilltops
and pink dog-roses. He died soon after becoming rector of the
Herefordshire parish of Bredwardine, a few miles downstream.

Extracts from *Kilvert's Diary*, first published in 1938.

*January 1, 6, 11, 12, 21, 25. February 2, 4, 6, 13, 22, 24.
March 1, 6, 10, 16, 19, 24. April 14, 15, 18, 22, 25, 27, 30.
May 2, 4, 9, 11, 18, 27. June 7, 9, 13, 15, 29, 30. July 9, 16,
22, 29. August 10, 11, 17, 25. September 5, 6, 8, 10, 14,
21, 24. October 4, 7, 9, 18, 25. November 3, 6, 8. December 8, 10, 15, 25, 27, 28, 31.*

D. H. LAWRENCE (1885–1930). Poet and novelist. Nottingham-
shire collier's son. Before his ultimate wanderings after the First
World War (Italy, Austria, Ceylon, Australia, Mexico, New
Mexico, France, etc.), he was variously in Buckinghamshire,
Sussex, Cornwall (St. Merryn, in January and February 1916;
then at Zennor, till October 1917), Berkshire, Derbyshire
(Middleton-by-Wirksworth).

Extracts from *The Letters of D. H. Lawrence.*

*January 5, 28. February 7, 9, 15, 24. March 8, 9. April 18, 30.
May 14, 23, 24. June 1, 3, 19, [27]. August 2. September 16.
November 9.*

KATHERINE MANSFIELD (1888–1923). Writer of stories, daughter
of a New Zealand banker. Her brief English life was variously
passed in London, Buckinghamshire, and Cornwall. She admired
Dorothy Wordsworth and the force of the small details of everyday
living which she recorded; and the writings of Colette.

Extracts from *The Letters of Katherine Mansfield*, 1928, and
Journal of Katherine Mansfield, 1954.

*January 4, 5, 20. February 1. May 16, 18. June 16, 21, 27.
September 30. December 28.*

JOHN EVERETT MILLAIS (1829–96). Painter, Pre-Raphaelite Brother, and eventually President of the Royal Academy. Extracts from a diary he kept (at the suggestion of Coventry Patmore, the poet) when he was twenty-two, and at work on his *Ophelia* and *The Huguenot*, at Worcester Park Farm, near Cheam, in Surrey, in the autumn and early winter of 1851. The diary is printed in his *Life and Letters*.

October 16. November 19, 29.

SAMUEL PALMER (1805–81). Painter and in his early years nature mystic. Son of a London bookseller, and friend of William Blake, in Blake's old age. He derived his visionary landscapes from the Kentish hills which are now concealed by the bricks and front gardens of Dulwich, and from the Kentish country near Sevenoaks and along the Darenth, by Lullingstone and Shoreham (where he lived in his most fertile years).

Extract from *Samuel Palmer: The Visionary Years.*

July 15.

SAMUEL PEPYS (1633–1703). Diarist and civil servant, of an old Fenland family (his father was for a time in the London tailoring trade), who became secretary to the Admiralty and president of the Royal Society. He was in the vigour of his late twenties and his thirties when he kept his *Diary*, filling it with the pleasures of food, drink, lute playing and singing, pretty women, the theatre, riding out in fine weather, and sleeping through sermons.

January 1, 16, 29. March 24. April 22. May 1, 13, 29. June 15, 28. July 13, 14, 16.

ANN RADCLIFFE (1764–1823). Novelist. She made summer tours from London with her journalist husband, recording the things they saw in a direct style which comes as a surprise after her stories of Gothick or romantic horror (*The Mysteries of Udolpho*, etc.).

Her journals do not seem to have survived in full: parts were printed with her posthumous romance *Gaston de Blondeville* (1826).

September 3, 21, 22, 23.

JOHN RUSKIN (1819–1900). Writer on art and society, and artist. London-born, brought up in Herne Hill when it was still in the

Surrey countryside. Lived out his life of sanity and unbalance in a house on Coniston Lake, in the Lake District.

Extracts from his *Diaries*, which mix egoism and petulance (when the weather is not what he wants) with clear perception.

> *January 17, 19, 31. February 16, 21, 25, 29. March 19, 26, 27, 28, 29. April 2, 4, 19, 21, 23. May 2, 22. June 16, 18, 28. July 1, 12, 26, 30. August 1, 7, 10, 13, 16, 20, 21, 22. September 20. October 14, 16, 30. November 2, 5, 11, 20, 22, 28, 30. December 3, 6, 23, 28.*

JAMES SMETHAM (1821–89). Artist, poet, and man of letters. Friend of Rossetti and Ruskin. Born at Pately Bridge, under the moors of Nidderdale in the West Riding. Also lived as a boy in Cheshire. His later home was Stoke Newington, then a Middlesex village unabsorbed by London. There in 1877 he was overtaken by melancholia.

Extracts from *The Letters of James Smetham*.

> *January 7. July 21. August 9, 23. November 1.*

GEORGE STURT (1863–1927). Schoolmaster, then owner of a family wheelwright's business in Farnham, Surrey, who wrote under the pseudonym of George Bourne. Influenced by Thoreau. His unsentimental books on labouring life and society and pre-industrial skills include *The Wheelwright's Shop* and *The Memoirs of a Surrey Labourer*.

Extracts from *The Journals of George Sturt, 1890–1903* (part only of the journals preserved in the British Museum).

> *March 4. April 7. November 21. December 1, 4, 17, 21.*

ALFRED TENNYSON (1809–92). The fourth of the twelve children of an unbalanced parson, who was rector of Somersby, under the Wolds, between Lincoln and the sad marshes of the Lady of Shalott and the sad North Sea. He walked and holidayed in Cornwall in search of detail for his Arthurian poems.

Extracts from *Tennyson: A Memoir*.

> *June 6, 8, 19. July 6, 8, 13. August 25.*

HORACE WALPOLE (1717–97). Miscellaneous writer, who made a profession of letter writing and friendship. Strawberry Hill, at Twickenham, which he turretted and cloistered and fitted out as a

'Gothic' home, was, in his day, completely in the Middlesex countryside, with unenclosed fields alongside.

Extracts from *Horace Walpole's Correspondence.*

June 6, 10, 11, 14. December 26.

GILBERT WHITE (1720–93). Bachelor cleric, most lucid and elegant writer on the natural history and antiquities of Selborne, in Hampshire, and one of the founders of English delight in natural history. At Selborne he was born (in his grandfather's vicarage), lived, died, and was buried; acting for more than twenty years as curate of a neighbouring parish.

Extracts from the *Journals of Gilbert White*, which he kept from 1768 to 1793. The entries are curt, yet add up to an extraordinary expression of the steady flow of life and the seasons.

January 1, 4, 7, 9, 13, 14, 16, 20, 22, 24. February 5, 6, 8, 15, 18, 19, 20. March 5, 7, 8, 14, 17, 18, 21, 22, 23, 25, 30, 31. April 1, 2, 3, 5, 8, 11, 16, 17, 24, 25. May 1, 5, 6, 8, 12, 13, 15, 16, 19, 24, 25, 26, 28, 31. June 1, 5, 7, 11, 12, 14, 20, 21, 22, 24, 27, 29. July 2, 4, 6, 8, 11, 12, 15, 17, 19, 20, 21, 25, 27, 28, 30, 31. August 3, 12, 15, 16, 23, 26, 30. September 4, 7, 9, 11, 15, 17, 19, 22, 23, 25, 30. October 3, 4, 8, 10, 13, 15, 23, 25, 26, 30. November 1, 2, 3, 4, 9, 13, 15, 16, 18, 19, 22, 23, 24, 25, 26, 27, 29. December 2, 4, 5, 11, 13, 14, 16, 21, 22, 25, 27, 30.

JAMES WOODFORDE (1740–1803). Guzzling bachelor cleric as egocentric as Gilbert White was the reverse. Son of a Somerset parson, and himself rector of Weston Longeville, along the Wensum, north-west of Norwich.

Extracts from his *Diary of a Country Parson, 1758–1802*, full both of gout and details of the over-eating which—had he known —was the cause of it.

January 14. February 1, 4, 18. April 11. May 1. June 19. November 6. December 25, 28.

DOROTHY WORDSWORTH (1771–1855). The supreme lyrical diarist. In the early diaries of her life with her brother, below the Quantocks and at Grasmere, she succeeds by never embroidering her report or overloading it with descriptive sentiment. She lived under her brother's roof for more than fifty years, in her younger days a plain brown-faced girl, awkward in movement, with the liveliest eyes. She became melancholic in later years.

185

Extracts from *The Journals of Dorothy Wordsworth*, 1941.

*January 23, 25, 26, 27, 29. February 1, 3, 7, 14, 17, 21,
24, 26, 27. March 1, 5, 12, 13, 18, 20, 21, 23, 24. April 6, 9,
12, 13, 15, 16, 17, 23, 29. May 1, 5, 6, 14, 16, 17, 20, 28, 31.
June 4, 9, 13, 16, 20, 23, 26. July 2, 4, 5, 7, 14, 15, 27, 31.
August 2, 4, 21, 22, 31. September 12, 14, 30. October 1, 2,
6, 7, 8, 11, 12, 30, 31. November 4, 7, 8, 10, 18, 24. December 12, 18, 19, 20, 21, 22, 24, 25, 29, 30.*

WILLIAM WORDSWORTH (1770–1850). Cumberland-born, and
always anxious to get back to the Lakes, in spite of happiness in
Dorset and Somerset. He and Dorothy came home to the North at
Christmas time 1799, settling into their rented, scantily furnished
cottage at Grasmere after a frosty, snowy, windy journey from
Teesdale on horseback, on foot, and by carriage.

The extract for December 24—from *The Early Letters of
William & Dorothy Wordsworth*—shows how his home took
possession of him.

December 24.